"In his typically clear and concise the Old Testament. As always, he passages chosen for *The Old Testament in Seven Sentences*, indeed, set the agenda for the drama of Scripture as it unfolds across the canon. This slim volume is yet another tool that Wright has produced to demonstrate the relevancy of the Old Testament. He is a gift to the church."

M. Daniel Carroll R. (Rodas), Blanchard Professor of Old Testament, Wheaton College and Graduate School

"*The Old Testament in Seven Sentences* sounds like an impossible task, but Chris Wright makes it work beautifully, capturing the central features of the Old Testament in a way that is both rich and accessible. I'm not surprised really—Wright is one of our best, most mature thinkers about the Bible today. His book gives readers an essential and impressive orientation to the life-giving message of the Old Testament. I recommend it highly."

Tremper Longman III, distinguished scholar and professor emeritus of biblical studies, Westmont College

"Wright's *The Old Testament in Seven Sentences* is a tour de force, capturing the heart of the Old Testament, its epic drama, and God's passion for his people with clarity and depth. Wright takes readers on a journey through the mountains and valleys of the Old Testament, sharing vistas of its beauty, its pain, and its picture of God's continuing plan of redemption and mission for God's people, culminating in Jesus Christ and the new creation of all things."

Beth Stovell, associate professor of Old Testament at Ambrose University, national catalyst for theological and spiritual formation for Vineyard Canada

"Christopher Wright has provided the church, seminary, and evangelist a creative and accessible tour of the biblical narrative. I commend this book as a resource for all who want to understand and be drawn into the Bible's story."

Chris Gonzalez, executive director of Missional Training Center, pastor of Missio Dei Communities

"What a fantastic title! What an imaginative project! What a delightful way into the Old Testament! What a great gift for anyone who is bewildered by the Old Testament and thinks they might be able to get into it if only they had some signposts!"

John Goldingay, professor of Old Testament, Fuller Theological Seminary

"Communicating the essence of the Old Testament to the Christian believer is a challenge. Christopher Wright has creatively met the challenge, summarizing its major themes under seven simple headings. These headings, beginning with creation and concluding with Psalms and Wisdom, lay out in easy-to-remember terms the history of salvation as it exists in the Old Testament and as it is fulfilled in Christ. With this as a guide, readers will find their way through an exciting but daunting journey, finding out how Jesus is the completion of the hope of Israel."

Duane Garrett, John R. Sampey Professor of Old Testament Interpretation, The Southern Baptist Theological Seminary

"This accessible, handy volume lifts the reader to a high-level narrative of God's work across the centuries and millennia, profound yet simplified, brief yet layered, condensed yet deep with a thought-provoking redemptive narrative. Read this Old Testament introduction, and you will be reminded of Scripture's common thread and the hope found in a purposeful God. Christopher J. H. Wright's easy, precise language and faithfulness to the biblical text combine to create a fresh, new classic."

Benjamin K. Homan, president of Langham Partnership USA (formerly John Stott Ministries)

THE OLD TESTAMENT

IN SEVEN SENTENCES

A SMALL INTRODUCTION TO A VAST TOPIC

CHRISTOPHER J. H. WRIGHT

IVP Academic

An imprint of InterVarsity Press
Downers Grove, Illinois

InterVarsity Press
P.O. Box 1400, Downers Grove, IL 60515-1426
ivpress.com
email@ivpress.com

InterVarsity Press® is the book-publishing division of InterVarsity Christian Fellowship/USA®, a movement of students and faculty active on campus at hundreds of universities, colleges, and schools of nursing in the United States of America, and a member movement of the International Fellowship of Evangelical Students. For information about local and regional activities, visit intervarsity.org.

All Scripture quotations, unless otherwise indicated, are taken from The Holy Bible, New International Version®, NIV®. Copyright © 1973, 1978, 1984, 2011 by Biblica, Inc.™ Used by permission of Zondervan. All rights reserved worldwide. www.zondervan.com. The "NIV" and "New International Version" are trademarks registered in the United States Patent and Trademark Office by Biblica, Inc.™

Some material in chapters 5 and 7 is condensed and adapted from Christopher J. H. Wright, How to Preach and Teach the Old Testament for All It's Worth *(Grand Rapids: Zondervan, 2016), also published as* Sweeter than Honey: Preaching the Old Testament *(Carlisle, UK: Langham Preaching Resources, 2016). Used with permission.*

Cover design: Bradley Joiner
Interior design: Beth McGill
Images: diagram of tabernacle by Daniel van Loon © InterVarsity Press

ISBN 978-0-8308-5225-3 (print)
ISBN 978-0-8308-7363-0 (digital)

Library of Congress Cataloging-in-Publication Data
Names: Wright, Christopher J. H., 1947- author.
Title: The Old Testament in seven sentences : a small introduction to a vast topic / Christopher J. H. Wright.
Description: Downers Grove, IL : IVP Academic, [2019] | Includes bibliographical references and index.
Identifiers: LCCN 2019002868 (print) | LCCN 2019009242 (ebook) | ISBN 9780830873630 (eBook) | ISBN 9780830852253 (pbk. : alk. paper) | ISBN 9780830873630 (digital)
Subjects: LCSH: Bible. Old Testament--Introductions. | Bible. Old Testament--Criticism, interpretation, etc.
Classification: LCC BS1140.3 (ebook) | LCC BS1140.3 .W75 2019 (print) | DDC 221.6/1--dc23
LC record available at https://lccn.loc.gov/2019002868

P	20	19	18	17	16	15	14	13	12	11	10	9	8	7	6	5	4	3	2	1
Y	36	35	34	33	32	31	30	29	28	27	26	25	24	23	22	21	20	19

To my colleagues

in

Langham Partnership

and the global family of "Langhamites"

All Chris Wright's royalties from this book have been irrevocably assigned to Langham Literature (formerly the Evangelical Literature Trust). Langham Literature is a program of the Langham Partnership International (LPI), founded by John Stott. Chris Wright is the International Ministries Director. Langham Literature distributes evangelical books to pastors, theological students, and seminary libraries in the Majority World, and fosters the writing and publishing of Christian literature in many regional languages. For further information on Langham Literature and LPI, visit langham.org.

CONTENTS

INTRODUCTION

Jesus got it down to two. Love God and love your neighbor—"all the Law and the Prophets hang on these two commandments" (Matthew 22:40).

Micah got it down to three. "To act justly and to love mercy and to walk humbly with your God" (Micah 6:8).

Even Moses got it down to five. Fear, walk, love, serve, obey . . . that's it (Deuteronomy 10:12-13).

So getting it down to seven should not be too hard.

That's what I thought, anyway. But then I wondered, as you might also, is it really right to condense the Scriptures in this way? After all, God gave us a pretty big library of books in the Bible, most of them in the Old Testament part. Paul insists that "all Scripture [meaning the Old Testament in his day] is God-breathed and useful" (2 Timothy 3:16). Ought we to be shortening it all into bite-size sentences and small chapters of explanation? Is a book about the Bible like this one *biblically* appropriate?

In addition to those three extreme examples above, there are quite a number of other places in the Bible itself where the whole message is trimmed down to a very condensed version, in order to make some of the crucial points crystal clear. Typically this is done by *telling the story*, or whatever part of it had happened by that time. For example:

- Moses summarizes the story so far in Deuteronomy 1–3 to urge greater obedience to God in the future.

- Israelite farmers are to recite the story as a way of affirming God's blessing and their own commitment to obey him (Deuteronomy 26:1-11).

- Joshua does it again with the next generation to urge them to go on choosing to serve their covenant God (Joshua 24).

- Two lengthy psalms, Psalms 105 and 106, tell the story again, showing how unfaithful Israel had been over the centuries and how much they owed, then and still, to the patience and grace of God.

- Nehemiah tells the whole story from creation to his own day as the basis for pleading with God for forgiveness and restoration of the people (Nehemiah 9:1-37).

- Jesus tells the story in the form of a parable about a vineyard and wicked tenants in a way that is very recognizable by those who oppose him (Matthew 21:33-46).

- Stephen tells the story, from Abraham to the crucifixion of Jesus, in a way that shows God's impatience with the constant rebellion of his people and enrages Stephen's listeners so much that they execute him for blasphemy (Acts 7:1-60).

- Paul tells the story (in almost seven sentences) in a rapid sequence that probably reflects his regular preaching and teaching: Abraham, exodus, land, judges, kings, David . . . and then straight to Jesus, Messiah and King (Acts 13:16-41).

What all these examples have in common, as I said, is that they do this summarizing work in narrative form. For that is essentially what the Old Testament (and indeed the whole Bible) is— the great story of the universe. All that the Old Testament has to teach us falls within the structure of that great story.

THE OLD TESTAMENT AS A LIBRARY

However, just before we fill out that story a little more, in relation to our seven sentences we should take note of the structure of the Old Testament as we have it in our English Bibles. It comes to us as a library of books, divided into several fairly clear sections or categories.

- *The Pentateuch* (a Greek word that means "five books"). These are the books from Genesis to Deuteronomy. The Bible calls this section the Torah. This word is often translated "the Law," but that is somewhat misleading. The word actually means "guidance" or "teaching," and although these books do contain laws that God gave to Israel, they also contain important narratives and a few songs and poems.

- *Historical books.* The books from Joshua to Esther give us the story of Israel, from the conquest of Canaan to the time after the Jews return from exile in Babylon—a period stretching from roughly 1200 to 450 BC.

- *Poetic books.* The books from Job to Song of Songs are a mixture of worship songs, wisdom texts, and a beautiful love poem.

- *Prophets.* Finally, the whole section from Isaiah to Malachi are books compiled from the preaching of those God raised up as prophets over a period of approximately three hundred years.

That is the order of the books in most modern Bibles. However, the order of books in the original Hebrew Scriptures, known as the canon, which Jews still use today and which would have been the order at the time of Jesus, is a little different. The whole library is divided into just *three* sections: the Law or Torah, the Prophets, and the Writings (or, as Jesus refers to the three sections, "the Law of Moses, the Prophets and the Psalms" [Luke 24:44]).

The Torah
- The Pentateuch (as above).

The Prophets
- The Former Prophets: Joshua, Judges, 1–2 Samuel, and 1–2 Kings (Jews regarded these as prophetic—that is, history told from God's point of view).
- The Latter Prophets: Isaiah, Jeremiah, Ezekiel, and the Book of the Twelve, from Hosea to Malachi.

The Writings
- Psalms, Job, Proverbs, Ruth, Song of Songs, Ecclesiastes, Lamentations, Esther, Daniel, Ezra, Nehemiah, and 1–2 Chronicles.

You can see from the table of contents that three of my seven sentences come from the Torah, one from the Former Prophets, two from the Latter Prophets, and one from the Writings.

THE OLD TESTAMENT AS A DRAMA

Let's come back to the point that the Old Testament fundamentally tells a story. To be more precise, it tells the essential first part of the great story that the whole Bible tells. To change the picture a bit, the Bible is not just story; it is like a great *drama*—an enormous play with a huge cast of actors, all playing their part in a vast narrative whose author and director is God himself. Here's the thing: we are not mere spectators, an audience in the theater of the Bible. No, we get to be part of the story; we become actors on stage. Indeed, we are called and commissioned to join the cast of God's drama and play our part in our own generation. We are in the Bible. Let me explain further.

Like most great dramas, the drama of the Bible is divided into several acts—that is, major sections of the story in which distinct and significant things take place as the drama moves forward. We can picture the whole Bible as a drama with seven acts.[1]

- *Act 1: Creation.* The whole drama begins when the one living and eternal God chooses to create what we call the universe— heaven and earth. He creates it "good," and he creates human beings in God's own image, to rule and serve his good creation.

- *Act 2: Rebellion.* Humans choose to distrust God's goodness, disbelieve God's word, and disobey God's instructions. As a result, sin and evil enter into every dimension of human life, personal and social, and also corrupt all cultures and bring damage and frustration to creation.

- *Act 3: Promise.* The story of the rest of the Old Testament begins with God's promise to Abraham that not only will he become a great nation (Israel), but also that through them God will bring blessing to all nations on earth. That promise and hope drives the story forward through the history of Israel in the Old Testament era, as we shall survey.

- *Act 4: Gospel.* The promise of the Old Testament comes to fulfillment when Jesus of Nazareth is born. The great central act of the drama of Scripture includes all that we read in the four Gospels: the conception, birth, life, teaching, atoning death, victorious resurrection, and ascension of Messiah Jesus.

- *Act 5: Mission.* The promise to Abraham must be fulfilled. The good news of what God has accomplished through his Son Jesus must go to all nations. This is launched at the end of the Gospels and the beginning of Acts, after the outpouring of the Spirit of God on the followers of Jesus.

- *Act 6: Final judgment.* The good news is that evil will not have the last word and God will ultimately put all things right (which is what judgment means in the Bible) by dealing with and destroying all that is wrong and evil. Act 6 is the completion of God's answer to act 2 and of the accomplishment of act 4.

- *Act 7: New creation.* The Bible drama ends with a dramatic new beginning! After putting all things right, God will make all things new and will come to dwell with redeemed humanity in his restored creation forever.

Seeing the whole Bible story in this way has many benefits.

First of all, it keeps us attached to the way God has chosen to give us the Bible itself—not merely as a book full of promises, rules, or doctrines (there are plenty of these in the Bible, but these are not what the Bible actually *is*), but in the form of a grand narrative with a beginning and an ending (actually a new beginning) and the whole redemptive plot in the middle.

Second, it reminds us that *this is our story*. For if we have come to be followers of the Lord Jesus Christ, then we are participants in act five of the drama of Scripture. That's where we are—somewhere between the resurrection of Christ and the return of Christ. In that place we have a role, a part to play, and a mission to accomplish, with God and for God.

Third, it shows us just how important the Old Testament is and how utterly wrong, misleading, and dangerous are those who tell Christians that they can happily ditch the Old Testament. This idea, which has become popular again (partly through sheer ignorance of the Bible and partly because of some high-profile preachers saying so), is not at all new. Less than a hundred years after Christ's resurrection, a man named Marcion tried to persuade the church that the God of the Old Testament was a completely different god from the God and Father of Jesus (that's where you heard it before, folks), and that the church should jettison the Old Testament and some parts of the New as well because they were too Jewish. The church rejected his teaching as wrong and heretical, and held on to the Old Testament Scriptures as a vital part of God's full revelation and therefore of the Christian canon of the Bible.

And as we survey the seven acts of the drama of Scripture, we can see how important it is that they did so. Without the first three acts, Jesus becomes just another human savior of some kind. The story would lose its essential beginning (creation), its profound problem (sin), and the governing theme of God's promise of blessing to all nations. If anyone suggests to you that you don't need the Old Testament (and probably shouldn't be reading this book), remind them that Jesus never read the New Testament, and the first Jesus followers (including the apostle Paul) went out into the world to evangelize, teach, and transform with only the Old Testament Scriptures at first—and did pretty well at it—until Paul started writing his letters and Mark produced his Gospel. Acts four through seven of the drama of Scripture all presuppose, build on, refer to, and quote the Scriptures that constitute acts one, two, and three. The whole story only makes sense *as* a whole story.

Why These Seven Sentences?

Let me offer a word about how I came to choose my seven sentences. The first three more or less chose themselves. We have to begin with creation, as the whole Bible does, and think about what the stories of Genesis 1–11 tell us about the world, God, ourselves, and our terrible plight as rebels against our Creator.

And then we have to move on to that triggering moment when God calls and chooses Abraham and gives him that promise that really governs the rest of the Bible—through the story of Israel, onward and outward to all nations in the whole earth. Paul calls our second sentence "the gospel" (Galatians 3:8).

From there we have to see the exodus as the greatest event of redemption in the Bible until the cross of Christ. In the same book we read about the covenant that God makes with Israel and the way of life that he calls the Israelites to observe (the law) in response to God's saving grace. But it is all based on what God has done for them—hence our third sentence.

The fourth was more difficult, since there is a huge chunk of history after the exodus. We can't ignore it, but we can't tell it in full—just a summary. However, in the middle of it comes the next most important covenant in the Bible—the one God makes with King David, since that points us eventually to King Jesus (as the apostle Paul was fond of saying). David grabbed the fourth sentence.

Having come that far, it seemed that we must tackle the great block of the books of the prophets. That seemed to split into two parts. Much of what the prophets have to say is challenging the people to turn back to God, to live in the way he wants, and warning them that if they do not do so, they will face horrendous judgment and destruction. Thus, for our fifth sentence I chose a well-known verse from Micah, one of those prophets who exposes the social depravity and injustice of the nation in contrast to what God truly wants from them. It is a verse that influenced Jesus also (Matthew 23:23) and inspires a lot of Christian ministry and mission today.

But the prophets also bring a message of hope beyond judgment. They have good news to share as they look into God's future, for Israel and for the world, as God will keep his promise through Israel for all the nations on earth. The New Testament word for "gospel" actually comes from the Old Testament (in the Greek translation that was often used in the days of Jesus and the other disciples, especially Paul). My sixth sentence is a gospel word about God's salvation, both for the exiles of Israel and also for "all the ends of the earth." It is a sentence that Paul quotes (Romans 10:15) and has inspired various hymns and songs.

The book of Psalms is probably still the favorite part of the Old Testament for many people, even those who never read much else in the rest of it. As I mentioned above, it is the primary book in the third section of the Hebrew canon, the Writings. It wasn't hard to choose as our seventh sentence what is also probably many people's favorite verse from their favorite psalm. And that provided a way to access both the book of Psalms itself and the Wisdom books in the same part of our Bible.

Finally, two small points before we plunge in. First, this is a short book, so although I do quote some essential texts, it isn't possible to lay out lengthy quotations of the biblical text. I hope you will enjoy just reading the book itself, but for best results, it really will be helpful, whenever convenient, to read the book with your Bible close at hand so that you can check out some of the references that I have scattered in to support the points being made. After all, the whole point of choosing these seven sentences is to encourage you to read a lot more of them in the Bible itself.

Second, after many years of teaching and writing on the Old Testament, it is not likely that what I think or write for a new book like this will be entirely new. I have taken the liberty of referring in the notes to bigger books by myself and others that can take you deeper and further if you want to. I am also particularly grateful to Zondervan Publishers and Langham Partnership for permission to condense and adapt in a few places in this book some material that was first published in my book *How to Preach and Teach the Old Testament for All It's Worth* (Grand Rapids: Zondervan, 2016), also published as *Sweeter than Honey: Preaching the Old Testament* (Carlisle, UK: Langham Preaching Resources, 2016).

- one -

CREATION

*In the beginning God created
the heavens and the earth.*

GENESIS 1:1

I t's a good place to start, don't you think? The first word of the
first sentence of the first part of the first book of the first
section of the First Testament—"In the beginning" (it's all one
word in Hebrew). Each of those firsts is important.

Our first word, translated "In the beginning," reminds us that
the Bible as a whole is a story, or rather *the* story—the true story
of the universe. The whole Bible begins with creation in Genesis
1–2, and it ends (or begins again) with the new creation in Revelation 21–22. And in between it narrates the vast, sprawling
narrative of how God has reconciled all things in heaven and
earth to himself through the Lord Jesus Christ.

The first book in the Bible is Genesis, the book of beginnings.
And the first part of the book, Genesis 1–11, tells us of the beginning of the world and the beginning of the nations of humanity. It tells us of the beginning of sin and evil within human
life and their effect on the earth itself. All of this is called the
Primal History, since it describes things that, although they

happened in a historical sense, cannot be placed in a precisely dated historical time frame. These people and events are primal in the sense that they come first, before the sort of recorded history to which we can give specific dates. Then, in the remainder of the book, Genesis 12–50, we read about the beginning of the people of Israel, through whom God promised to bring blessing into that world of nations and to heal their fractured relationship with God.

The first section of the Old Testament, starting here, comprises the five books of Genesis, Exodus, Leviticus, Numbers, and Deuteronomy. These five books are the foundation block of the whole Old Testament—indeed, of the whole Bible. In historical terms, they take us from the creation of the universe to the moment when the people of Israel reach the borders of the land God promised them. In terms of our seven acts of the great drama of Scripture (see the introduction), they take us through acts one and two and then launch us into act three.

KNOWING THE STORY WE ARE IN

The point about the Bible being one whole big story (or metanarrative) is that it provides our worldview as Christians. A worldview is the way we look at life, the universe, and everything. It is the lens of assumptions through which we interpret all that surrounds us in our daily lives, consciously or (more often) unconsciously within our cultures. Worldviews are formed from the answers given to certain key questions that all human beings ask and answer in some way. Here are four such worldview questions:

1. *Where are we?* What is the material universe we see around us? Where did it come from, or has it always been here? Is it real? Why and how does it exist, and does it have any purpose or destiny?

2. *Who are we?* What does it mean to be human? Are we just the same as the rest of the animals on this planet or different from them in some way? What (if anything) makes us special or unique? Why are we the dominant species, and is that a good or bad thing?

3. *What's gone wrong?* Universally, humans believe that things are not how they are supposed to be, or at least not what they could or should be. We live in the midst of a world gone wrong, between ourselves and between us and the natural order. Why is this? What caused this wrongness to be the dominant reality of human life on earth?

4. *What's the solution?* Universally, humans also seem to believe that things *could* be fixed and made better, and all kinds of solutions are proposed—by religions and philosophies, by politicians and reformers, even by revolutionaries and anarchists. Who is right? Is there anything we can do to solve the human predicament? Is there any escape, or salvation, from the mess we are in? Is there any hope for the world?

Whether you are a Muslim, a Hindu, a Buddhist, or a secular modern atheist, you will ask and answer these questions, in different ways according to the narrative of reality that you hold—the great story that you and your culture tells. But if you are a Jew or a Christian, you will answer all of these questions from the Scriptures. For a Christian that means the overarching story of both Testaments of the Bible. It is the Bible that tells us where we are, who we are, what's gone wrong, what's the solution—and points to a future filled with hope. It gets on with that job very quickly: the Bible sketches in answers to the first three of those fundamental questions within the first three chapters of the Old Testament, expands on the third question for a while in the rest of Genesis 4–11, and then goes on to launch God's answer to the fourth question in Genesis 12. In other words, the Bible answers those fundamental worldview questions by telling us the true story from the very beginning. Here is the setting (God's creation), the characters (God and the human race), the problem (evil, sin, death), and here is the promise of a solution (through Israel and the Messiah, Jesus).

It will take the rest of the Bible to fill out those answers in multiple ways, of course. But the basic framework of the biblical worldview is set out in the first quarter of Genesis. Here is God's executive summary of his big book, if you like.

WHERE ARE WE?

We look around ourselves as humans and wonder at the astonishing environment of our lives. We look up at skies, clouds, birds, sun, moon, stars. We look around at mountains, rivers, forests, oceans, deserts. We look down at soil, crops, animals wild and domesticated, insects, depths of earth and sea, fish and creatures of the deep. Maybe, with Louis Armstrong, we think to ourselves, "What a wonderful world!"—and it is. Awe, fear, admiration, curiosity, gratitude, affection, surprise, expectancy—all these arise in our response to simply being in this world. And the questions arise: Where did all these things come from? Who or what made them? Who or what controls them? How should we relate to them for best results?

Israel lived in a world of nations that had plenty of answers to those questions. The stories of the ancient Near East (especially in Egypt and Babylon) attributed the origins of the natural world to a variety of gods, whose squabbles and needs (mirroring their very human inventors) produced this or that feature of the universe. Certain features of the earth matched the demand of the gods for a home, or temple, within which human beings could serve their needs. Others resulted from battles between deities when things got split apart.[1]

In clear and conscious distinction from these surrounding stories, Genesis 1 tells us where we are. We inhabit the dry land of the earth, which owes its existence to the one single Creator God, along with the seas, the skies above, and the swarming creatures that fill these three great spaces of land, sea, and sky. This one God created all these massive entities and abundant creatures solely by his own powerful word, not in collaboration or conflict with any other deities. This affirmation leads to some vast additional truths about the creation in which we live.

Creation is distinct from God but dependent on God. Our sentence for this chapter, "In the beginning God created the heavens and the earth," tells us that there is a fundamental onto-logical distinction between God as Crea*tor* and everything else as creat*ed*.[2] The heavens and the earth had a beginning. God was there before the beginning. God and the universe are different in their being. This *duality* between the creator and the created is essential to all biblical thought and a Christian worldview. It stands against both monism (the belief that all reality is One, with no differentiation—as in Advaita Hinduism) and pantheism (the belief that God is somehow identical with the totality of the universe; everything in nature put together is God). This biblical teaching stands against New Age spiritualities, which adopt a broadly monistic or pantheistic worldview.

Creation, then, is distinct from God its Creator, but it is also totally dependent on God. Creation is not independent or coeternal. The world is not, in biblical teaching, a self-sustaining biosystem. Rather, God is actively and unceasingly sustaining its existence and its functions at macro and micro levels (Psalms 33:6-9; 65:9-13; 104; Colossians 1:17; Hebrews 1:3). This is not to deny that God has built into the earth an incredible capacity for renewal, recovery, balance, and adaptation. But the way in which all these systems work and interrelate is itself planned and sustained by God.

Creation is good. This is the unmistakable message of the opening chapter of the Bible. Six times God declares what he has just done to be "good," and the seventh time "very good." At least three things follow from this volley of goods.

1. The good creation reveals the good God. In other ancient Near Eastern accounts, creation is the work of multiple deities, in varying degrees of conflict and malevolence. By contrast, in the Old Testament creation is the work of the one single living God and therefore bears witness to his existence, power, and character. Creation reveals its Creator, though he is not part of it. Just as you can hear Beethoven in his symphonies (though a symphony is not the composer), or see Rembrandt in his paintings (though a painting is not the artist), so we encounter the living God in creation (though the creation is not God). Creation has a living voice that speaks for God.

We learn that the heavens declare the glory of God, without human speech but a voice that is heard to the ends of the earth (Psalm 19:1-4). Furthermore, "the heavens proclaim his righteousness, for he is a God of justice" (Psalm 50:6). It is not only farmers who care for the land. God does so continuously as evidence of his generosity (Psalm 65:9). It is not only humans who receive their food ultimately from God's hand; so do all creatures (Psalm 104:27-30). Paul points to the kindness of God on the evidence of his gifts of rain and crops, food and joy (Acts 14:17). He affirms that all human beings can see the evidence of God's existence and power in the creation of the world (Romans 1:20).

2. Creation is good in God's sight. The repeated affirmation "God saw that it was good" is made quite independently of us human beings. It is not initially *our human* response to the beauty or benefits of creation (though it certainly should be) but *God's* evaluation of God's own handiwork. It is the seal of God's approval on the whole universe in all its functioning. Creation has intrinsic value because it is valued by God, who is the source of all value. To speak of the goodness of creation is not, first of all, to say that it is valuable to us (which of course it is), but to say that it is valued by God and was created fit for purpose—God's purpose.

Psalm 104 celebrates not only those aspects of creation that serve human needs (crops and domestic animals) but also those that have no immediate connection with human life—the wild places and wild creatures that live there, simply being and doing what God created them to be and do. They are good too, because God values them.

3. Creation is good as God's temple. In the ancient world generally, temples were envisaged as (literally) microcosms—that is, small representations or replicas on earth of the shape and order of the cosmos itself. A temple was where heaven and earth came together. Meanwhile the cosmos could be seen as a macro-temple—that is, the dwelling place of the gods (or in Old Testament terms, of course, of the one, true, living Creator God).[3]

From this perspective, when God says that his work of creation is good, it is a way of saying that he sees and approves the whole creation, functioning in all its ordered complexity both as the place prepared for him to install his image (humankind) and as the place for his own dwelling ("Heaven is my throne, and the earth is my footstool," Isaiah 66:1-2—temple language). That is why the imagery of the new creation at the very end of the Bible speaks of the whole of heaven and earth as the dwelling place of God.

Creation is God's property. "The earth is the LORD's" (Psalm 24:1). "To the LORD your God belong the heavens, even the highest heavens, the earth and everything in it" (Deuteronomy

10:14). These are staggering universal affirmations that we easily slip past. The whole universe (including planet Earth) is God's property. It belongs to him. The earth is first and foremost owned by God, not by us. God is the supreme landlord. We are God's tenants, living by God's permission in God's property.[4] This generates huge ethical implications for our ecological and economic activity, which we can't go into here. But at the very least it reminds us that we are accountable to God for how we treat his property. And if we say that we love God, we should treat what belongs to God with respect and responsibility (as we would the property of anyone we love).

From its very first sentence the Bible constantly speaks of the natural world in relation to God. The created order obeys God, reveals his glory, benefits from his provision, serves his purposes (in judgment or salvation), and is filled with his presence. We honor creation as sacred in that sense—not as something divine in itself, not as something we are to worship (that is explicitly forbidden; see Deuteronomy 4:15-20; Job 31:26-28; Romans 1:25), but because it is related to God in every dimension of its existence.

This is where we are: in God's good creation, tenants in God's property, images of God in God's temple.

WHO ARE WE?

This is God's earth, then. But it is also our earth. "The highest heaven belongs to the LORD, but the earth he has given to mankind" (Psalm 115:16). The earth is the place of human habitation. It is God's property, but it is also our responsibility. The earth is in some sense given to human beings in a way that it is not given to other animals. So who are we?

What makes us humans special or unique? At first glance, the Bible stresses much more what we have in common with the rest of the animals than anything different from them.

- We are blessed and told to multiply—but so were they, and before us.

- We are created "on the sixth day"—but only after the other wild and domestic animals.

- We are created from the ground, as they were, or rather "from the dust of the ground" (Genesis 2:7), which hardly makes us superior.

- We are given the "breath of life"—but so were all the living creatures that breathe (Genesis 1:30; 6:17; 7:18, 22; Psalm 104:29-30).

- We are provided with food by God—but so are they (Genesis 1:29-30).

In fact it is a matter of wonder and rejoicing that we share with all the other animals in the love, care, and provision of God (Psalm 104:14-30). We are *'adam* from the *'adamah* (like humans from the humus, a word meaning "the organic component of soil"). We are all creatures of the Creator God, and that is wonderful.

What, then, makes us different? Three things are affirmed in Genesis: we were created in the image of God in order to be equipped to exercise dominion within creation (Genesis 1:26-28); we were placed in the earth (initially in the garden in Eden) in order to serve and care for it (Genesis 2:15); and we were created male and female to help one another in these huge responsibilities (Genesis 1:27; 2:18-25). Let's look at each of these in turn.

Created to rule (Genesis 1:26-28): kings, in the image of God.

Then God said, "Let us make mankind in our image, in our likeness, so that they may rule over the fish in the sea and the birds in the sky, over the livestock and all the wild animals, and over all the creatures that move along the ground."

> So God created mankind in his own image,
>> in the image of God he created them;
>> male and female he created them.
>
> God blessed them and said to them, "Be fruitful and in-
> crease in number; fill the earth and subdue it. Rule over the
> fish in the sea and the birds in the sky and over every living
> creature that moves on the ground."

The grammar of these verses implies that God creates human
beings *with the intention* that they should exercise rule over the
rest of the animal creation, and that he creates us in the image of
God in order to equip us for that function. The two things (image
of God and dominion over creation) are not identical with each
other, but they are closely related: the first enables the second.[5]

We were created to exercise the delegated kingship of God
within creation. Just as emperors set up statues (images) of
themselves in the countries they ruled to indicate their authority
over those realms, so human beings as the image of God represent the authority of the real king.

But how does God exercise his kingship within creation? The
Psalms tell us. Psalm 104 says that God does so by caring and
providing for all his creatures, wild, domestic, and human. Psalm
145 (which is addressed to "my God the King") says that God
rules by being gracious, good, faithful, generous, protective, and
loving toward all he has made.

That is how *God* is king. Therefore, human rule in creation
was never a license to dominate, abuse, crush, waste, or destroy.
That is tyranny modeled on fallen human arrogance, not kingship
modeled on God's character and behavior. The true model of
kingship is summarized in 1 Kings 12:7 ("If today you will be a
servant to these people and serve them"): mutual servanthood.
The people will serve the king—yes, provided he will serve and

care for them without injustice. The earth will serve our needs—yes, provided we exercise our kingship in God's way by serving and caring for it.

Located to serve (Genesis 2:15): priests, in the service of creation. This follows naturally from the point above. God takes the man he has created and puts him in the garden (literally) "to work it and take care of it." Human rule within creation (Genesis 1) is to be exercised by human servanthood for creation (Genesis 2). The pattern of servant-kingship is very clear, and it is modeled perfectly of course by Jesus himself, the perfect human and the Son of God, when he deliberately demonstrates his status as Lord and Master by washing the disciples' feet. Kingship exercised in servanthood: that is Christ's way, and it should be ours too.

But the language of serving and keeping has another resonance. It is the language of priesthood. Repeatedly in Leviticus it is said that the task of the priests and Levites is to serve God in the tabernacle/temple and keep all that God has entrusted to them there. We have, then, a priestly role as well as a kingly role within creation. We have authority to rule, and we have responsibility to serve.

Thus, the language of God placing his image (human beings) within creation has temple overtones as well, for that is where the images of the gods were indeed placed—in their temples. With the cosmos functioning as the macrotemple of its Creator, God places his own image—the living human being—in his temple to dwell with him there. Creation functions as the dwelling place of God, and human beings function as the image of God, ruling and serving creation on his behalf.

Created in relationship, male and female, for our task in creation. The first two chapters of Genesis give us two different but quite complementary portrayals of what it means to be male and female.

Genesis 1, on the one hand, tells us that for human beings being male and female is closely linked to being created in God's image.

> So God created mankind in his own image,
> in the image of God he created him;
> male and female he created them. (Genesis 1:27)

The way this verse is structured, with its tight parallelism, shows that there is something about our gender complementarity (male and female) that reflects something true about God. That's to say, being male and female *humans* means more than just enabling us to mate and reproduce like the rest of the animals. Human sexuality is part of what it means to be the image of God (says the verse). Not that God is gendered or sexually differentiated, but that *personal relationship* is part of the essential nature of God and therefore also part of the essential nature of humanity, since we were created in his image. Human sexual complementarity and the personal relationships it enables reflect *within the created order* something that is true about God within his uncreated, divine being.

Genesis 2, on the other hand, sets our maleness and femaleness in the context of the human task, as described above. God has called his whole creation "good" and "very good." It comes as a shock, then, when he announces that something is "not good" (Genesis 2:18). What is not good is that the man (the "earth creature") should be alone. But in the immediate context, the problem of this aloneness is not merely that he would therefore be lonely, in an emotional sense. God is addressing not merely a psychological problem but a creational one.

God has given an immense task to this creature in Genesis 2:15. He has been put in the garden "to work it and take care of it." When we add this to the task specified in the earlier creation account—to "fill the earth and subdue it" and to rule over the rest of the animate creation (Genesis 1:28)—the human task seems limitless. A man cannot tackle such a challenge alone. That is "not good." He needs help. God sets out, not to find him a *companion* to stop him feeling lonely, but to find a "*helper* to stand alongside and equal to" him in this huge task laid on him as the servant, keeper, filler, subduer, and ruler of creation. The man doesn't just need company. He needs help.[6] Male and female are necessary, not only for mutual relationship in which they will reflect God (though certainly for that), but also for mutual help in carrying out the creation mandate entrusted to humanity.

Humanity, then, is created in relationship, for relationship, and for a task that requires relational cooperation—not only at the basic biological level that only a man and a woman can produce children in order to fill the earth, but also at the wider societal level that both men and women have their roles of mutual assistance in the great task of ruling the creation on God's behalf.

WHAT'S GONE WRONG?

Things do not continue as God intended. Sin enters human life through rebellion and disobedience. The profound simplicity of the narratives of Genesis 3–11 shows us at least three things about sin that the rest of the Bible presupposes and demonstrates in so many ways.

Sin infects every part of life for every human being. The opening chapters of Genesis tell us more about ourselves as human beings as well as that we are created in God's image for the reasons mentioned above.

Human beings are *physical* (we are creatures in the created physical world); *spiritual* (we have a unique intimacy of relationship with God); *rational* (we have unique powers of communication, language, addressability, consciousness, memory, emotions, and will); and *social* (being male and female reflects the relational dimension of God and underlies all human relationships). All of these dimensions are combined in the integrated human person. They are not different parts that can be separated but different dimensions of the whole person.

The story of the temptation of Eve (with Adam's collusion—he is there "with her"; see Genesis 3:6) involves all four of these dimensions of human life, showing how sin enters into all of them.

> Now the serpent was more crafty than any of the wild animals the Lord God had made. He said to the woman, "Did God really say, 'You must not eat from any tree in the garden'?"
>
> The woman said to the serpent, "We may eat fruit from the trees in the garden, but God did say, 'You must not eat fruit from the tree that is in the middle of the garden, and you must not touch it, or you will die.'"
>
> "You will not certainly die," the serpent said to the woman. "For God knows that when you eat from it your eyes will be opened, and you will be like God, knowing good and evil."
>
> When the woman saw that the fruit of the tree was good for food and pleasing to the eye, and also desirable for gaining wisdom, she took some and ate it. She also gave some to her husband, who was with her, and he ate it. (Genesis 3:1-6)

• Spiritually, Eve begins to doubt the truth and goodness of God, undermining her trust and obedience.

• Mentally, she contemplates the fruit of the tree of the knowledge of good and evil: her thinking is rational (it is good for food), aesthetic (it is pleasing to the eye), and intellectual (it is desirable for gaining wisdom). All these capacities of the human mind are good in themselves. Indeed, the Bible commends them as good gifts of God. There is nothing wrong with Eve using her mind; the problem is she is now using all its powers *in a direction that was forbidden by God*. The problem is not rationality but disobedience.

- Physically, "she took and ate." These simple verbs describe physical action in the physical world. She uses her hands and mouth to commit an act of disobedience.

- Socially, she shares the fruit with Adam, "who was with her." Adam goes along with it. He hears the conversation but does nothing to challenge it. And so the sin that is already spiritual, mental, and physical also becomes shared—it enters into the core of human relationship, producing shame and fear.

The Bible will go on to show how sin continues to corrupt these same four dimensions of human life and experience.

- Spiritually, we are alienated from God, fearful of God's presence, suspicious of God's truth, and hostile to God's love.

- Rationally, we use our minds, like the first human couple, to rationalize and justify our sin, blame others, and excuse ourselves. We have become darkened in our thinking.

- Physically, we are sentenced to death, as God decreed, and suffer death's invasion through sickness and decay even in life itself, while our whole physical environment likewise groans in futility under God's curse.

- Socially, human life is fractured at every level, with anger, jealousy, violence, and murder even between brothers in the story of Cain and Abel escalating into the horrendous social decay and international strife that the rest of the biblical narrative graphically portrays.

Romans 1:18-32 is Paul's incisive commentary on the universal reign of sin in human life and society. Reading his searing analysis, we can see all of the same four dimensions of human personality involved in human sin and rebellion. There is no part of the human person that is unaffected by sin. Sin is a kind of power that exercises its dominion over us—until it is defeated by Christ on the cross.

Sin affects the earth. When human beings choose to rebel against their Creator, their disobedience and fall affects the whole of their physical environment. This is immediately clear from God's words to Adam, "Cursed is the ground because of you" (Genesis 3:17). This was inevitable. We are not only part of the whole interdependent system of life on earth; we are the dominant species. When humanity rebels against God, the rest of the created order suffers the effect. Not only are we alienated from God; not only are we alienated from an environment that often seems hostile and resistant; but also the earth itself is subject to frustration, as Paul also puts it—unable to freely and fully glorify God as it was created to do, until both we and it are liberated from that curse (Romans 8:19-23).

These early chapters of Genesis show that the problem is not only sinful human beings living in rebellion against God, but also the cursed earth that is the location of their evil and contributing to their suffering. For example, when Lamech (the one descended from Seth, not Cain) has a son, he names him Noah (which means "rest" or "comfort"), saying, "He will comfort us in the labor and painful toil of our hands caused by the ground the Lord has cursed" (Genesis 5:29). That is the longing of humanity—for God to lift the curse on the earth. It does not happen in the lifetime of Lamech's son, however (it will not happen until the end of the story, in Revelation 22:3). On the contrary, God's judgment falls in the form of the flood, specifically on the earth

WHAT DOES THE CURSE ON THE GROUND REFER TO?

I do not think that we should regard the fall of humanity into sin and God's curse on the earth as the cause of all the phenomena in nature that can be threatening to human life, if we are around when they happen (earthquakes, floods, volcanoes, tsunamis, etc.). Those natural processes, when the tectonic plates of the earth's crust shift, are and always have been part of the way this planet is structured—long before human beings arrived and fell into sin. More than that, they are a necessary part of the conditions for human life (all life on earth, in fact). Without the shifting of tectonic plates there would be no mountains. Without mountains there would be no precipitation, rivers, and variable climate. Without volcanoes, rivers, and floods, there would be no fertile soil. These are geological and climatic realities. We can hardly dictate to God how he ought to have made the world.[7]

I think the curse on the ground refers to the soil, the surface of the earth on which we live and depend (that is the common meaning of the word *'adamah* in Genesis 3:17), rather than to the whole planet. It is a functional curse, in which our human relationship with the earth we live on is radically distorted by sin and evil. The earth fights back. We have to sweat and toil just to eat bread. At one level, the curse on the earth is a way of describing the obvious fact that we humans are at odds with our natural environment, in multiple ways that harm both us and it.

But also, Paul tells us that creation itself is frustrated in its primary function to glorify God (Romans 8:20). Yes, as the Psalms say, creation does still declare the glory of God, but it cannot (yet) do so as fully as God intended because it is subject to the same kind of futility and frustration that blights human life also through our sin and rebellion. But the great good news (the gospel) of the whole Bible story is that *creation as a whole* is included in God's great plan of salvation. Our destiny in Christ is not to be saved *out of the earth* and go somewhere else, but rather to be saved, redeemed, *along with the whole creation*, which has been reconciled to God through the blood of Christ shed on the cross. (Psalm 96:11-13; Isaiah 65:17-25; Romans 8:18-25; Ephesians 1:9-10; Colossians 1:15-20; Revelation 21–22). And in that new creation, "No longer will there be any curse" (Revelation 22:3).

and its creatures as well as on sinful humanity (Genesis 6:6-7, 13, 17). Sin brings God's judgment on creation as well as humanity—for we are bound together. We are bound together also when God's grace brings salvation to creation as well as humanity—but that's the longer story.

Sin permeates human society and history. The narrative of Genesis 4–11 grinds on with increasing wickedness. The first family sees the eruption of jealousy, anger, and murder between brothers (Cain and Abel). The generations after Cain mix cultural development with boasting and escalating violence (Genesis 4:19-24). Generations pass, with the tolling bell of death terminating every one of them, no matter how long their lives (Genesis 5). The whole of human society becomes a mass of violence and corruption (Genesis 6:5, 11-13). Even after the purging waters of the flood and the emergence of a fresh start for creation, with God's words of blessing echoing Genesis 1, sin rebounds again in the family of Noah (Genesis 9:18-29). And the primal narrative reaches its climax at Babel, with the whole world of nations confused, divided, and scattered across the face of the earth (Genesis 11:1-9).

The picture is two dimensional: sin spreads horizontally within society, and sin escalates vertically between generations. Human life and cultures become increasingly laden with collective sin. That collective sin somehow consolidates into a power or force that is much more than the fact that all of us individually are sinners. Sin becomes endemic, structural, and embedded in history. The history books of the Old Testament tell the lurid story of how things get worse and worse in Israel as generations go by. The prophets see not only the sin of individuals but also the way society as a whole has become rotten and corrupt. Isaiah, for example, attacks those who legalize injustice by passing laws that give structural legitimacy to oppression:

Woe to those who make unjust laws,
  to those who issue oppressive decrees,
to deprive the poor of their rights
  and withhold justice from the oppressed of my people.
    (Isaiah 10:1-2)

Every king in Jerusalem seems to be worse than the one before (with very few exceptions, such as Hezekiah and Josiah) until the weight of accumulated evil became simply intolerable to God.

These stories in the Primal History, then, contain enormous depths of truth about the triangle of relationships between God, humanity, and the whole created order. The Bible offers us a radical and profound assessment of the effects of our willful rebellion and fall into disobedience, self-centeredness, and sin. It is not just that every dimension of the human person is affected by sin. It is not just that every human person is a sinner. It is also the case that our social and economic relationships with each other, horizontally and historically, and our ecological relationship to the earth itself have all been perverted and twisted by our collective sin, our idolatry, and our collusion with satanic powers of evil.

WHAT'S THE SOLUTION?

The answers to our first three questions have produced a vast problem on a cosmic scale. We live in God's creation, but we have spoiled it with our sin. We are made in God's image, but we fail to reflect the character of God. We live as a multitude of nations and cultures, but we have used ethnic diversity as a cause of hatred, violence, and injustice among nations. We are individually sinful and disobedient to the God who created us, provides for us, and loves us. We are, as Paul says, slaves to the dominion of sin. In all of these dimensions, the whole earth stands under the judgment of God.

If there is to be any solution to these desperate predicaments, it cannot come from us. We are too radically flawed to provide the answer to our own mess, as millennia of human history have demonstrated. It is important to see that the Bible portrays this whole problem, not by asking the question, "How can we all get to heaven when we die?" Our texts do not talk about the need for us to go somewhere else to be with God and how can we do that, since we are so sinful. The problem is, How can the holy and loving Creator God once again dwell in harmony with the humans he created in his own image in the midst of the earth that is now subject to God's curse? How can we be and do within God's creation what we were created to be and do? How can God once again walk and talk with us in the garden, now that we are rebels against him? That is the problem the whole Bible addresses—and ultimately solves, since the grand climactic vision of the Bible is not about us all going somewhere else ("up to heaven") but about *God coming here to dwell with us*, with all those redeemed by the blood of Christ from every nation, in the unified heaven and earth of the new creation, purged of all sin and evil.

This is the solution that God alone provides, since we cannot. It is the solution that the whole Bible story, centered on the death and resurrection of Jesus Christ, will present as gospel, as good news. And it is the solution that will address all three of those great needs: the sinfulness of every individual, the brokenness of the nations, and the curse and frustration of the earth. There are hints and signposts of these things in the Primal History, but we can see them more clearly in the light of what follows, in our next chapter.

two

ABRAHAM

All peoples on earth will be
blessed through you.

GENESIS 12:3

Human beings are radically flawed and living in sinful rebellion against God. The ground we live on is cursed, and
creation is detrimentally affected by our sin. The nations are
scattered and confused. It's a massive problem. And by the time
we reach Genesis 11, we might be wondering, "What can God do
next? Is there any hope for humanity and the earth?"

Actually, even within the Primal History, God has already
given hints that sin and evil will not have the last word—for the
human race, the earth, or the nations. God has plans for all three.

In Genesis 3:15, God assures the serpent that, though there
will be enmity between his offspring and the woman's (that is,
destructive conflict between the world of satanic evil and the
human race), in the end it will be a human being (offspring of
the woman) who will crush the serpent's head. God guarantees
victory over the source of evil and temptation. God will ensure
that the human race will not ultimately be destroyed by all that

the serpent represents. This verse is sometimes called the *proto-evangelium*, meaning "first gospel," the first announcement of the good news that God will win the victory over Satan through a human being. We know, of course, that it will ultimately be fulfilled through the man Jesus of Nazareth. But here in its context, it is simply a declaration of hope for humanity's ultimate future based on God's assertion of victory over the serpent. God will win, and he will do so through a human being.

In Genesis 8:15–9:17, God brings Noah and his family and all the animals out of the ark for what is effectively a fresh start for creation itself (notice the echoes of Genesis 1 in Genesis 8:17; 9:1, 7). For the first time in the biblical record, God makes a covenant, a solemn promise and commitment. Most significantly, it is not a covenant with Noah only (even though it is usually called the Noahic covenant) but a covenant with all life on earth. The phrase "every living creature on earth" is repeated several times. God's promise is, negatively, that he will never again destroy the earth with a flood, and positively, that he will preserve the conditions for life on earth for as long as the earth endures. And this, says God, is an "everlasting covenant." There is hope for the earth, as well as for humankind. God's judgment has fallen on both; now his covenant promise embraces both.

But wait. Here's the problem. God promises never to destroy the earth or the human race on it, and yet in the same breath God says, "for every inclination of the human heart is evil from childhood" (Genesis 8:21).[1] But if God knows how profoundly sinful humans are, how can that not lead inevitably again to judgment and destruction? Surely it must do so—unless God has some other plan. And very soon (in Genesis 12), we will discover that God has exactly that.

In Genesis 11, the story of the Tower of Babel, the confusion of languages is at one level an act of divine judgment. Yet, in

God's own speech in Genesis 11:6-7, it is intended to prevent something worse.

> Now the whole world had one language and a common speech. As people moved eastward, they found a plain in Shinar and settled there.
>
> They said to each other, "Come, let's make bricks and bake them thoroughly." They used brick instead of stone, and tar for mortar. Then they said, "Come, let us build ourselves a city, with a tower that reaches to the heavens, so that we may make a name for ourselves; otherwise we will be scattered over the face of the whole earth."
>
> But the Lord came down to see the city and the tower the people were building. The Lord said, "If as one people speaking the same language they have begun to do this, then nothing they plan to do will be impossible for them. Come, let us go down and confuse their language so they will not understand each other."
>
> So the Lord scattered them from there over all the earth, and they stopped building the city. (Genesis 11:1-8)

God can foresee what might be the result of human arrogance and their frustration of God's plans. It is clear from Genesis 9–10 that God's intention was that human beings should multiply and spread out (scatter) across the earth. Genesis 11 portrays a halt to that as the people choose to settle in one place, build a tower, make a name for themselves, and *avoid being scattered* as God intended. God perceives that such collective arrogance would be disastrous, and history shows that when humans try to create a uniform, totalitarian structure for their lives, it always ends in tyranny and misery. Thus, God confuses and scatters, as much as a preventative measure as a punitive one. The scattering over the face of the earth is what God intended anyway. The confusion of language prevents the human race from achieving complete unity *while we are still in our state of arrogance, sin, and rebellion.* God has better plans for the nations of the world, plans that will preserve their ethnic, cultural, and linguistic diversity ("every nation, tribe, people and language," Revelation 7:9), and yet will also unify them, not in united rebellion against God, but in united worship of God and the Lamb of God.

The Primal History ends with huge problems portrayed and unresolved, but with God still very much in charge, having given notice that humanity's sin will not ultimately defeat God's good purposes for God's good creation.

But still, we ask again, what can God do next?

Enter Abraham and Sarah (actually Abram and Sarai, but we know them better by the names God gives them a little later in the story).

GOD'S CALL AND PROMISE TO ABRAHAM AND SARAH

Genesis 12 comes after Genesis 11. Knowing that won't get you a PhD, but it is vitally important in understanding what comes next in the Bible story. For it is against the background of the bleak stories told in Genesis 3–11 that we must see the significance of God's intervention in the life of this man Abraham.

Those stories have told us that the earth lies under God's curse, that some people tried (and failed) to make a great name for themselves, and that the nations are spreading out over all the earth. When God calls Abraham, it is in order to initiate a project that will bring blessing instead of curse, that will make Abraham's name great (not Babel's), and that will eventually spread (though Abraham's people) to all the nations on earth. In other words, we must see Genesis 12 as the beginning of the story that answers the problems outlined in Genesis 1–11.

In examinations, the questions on the exam paper can be quite short, but the answers need to be rather longer. Looking at the Bible, we could say that Genesis 12–Revelation 22 is God's long answer to the question set in Genesis 1–11: What can God do about the brokenness of humanity, the earth, and the nations?

The story begins when Abraham's father, Terah, takes his family north from Ur (in what is now southern Iraq) to Harran (probably in what is now northeast Syria), and settles there for a while (Genesis 11:27-32). From there God calls Abraham to get up and go, trusting in God's promise. The words are rightly famous and conclude with this chapter's sentence.

> The LORD had said to Abram, "Go from your country, your people and your father's household to the land I will show you.
>
> > "I will make you into a great nation,
> > and I will bless you;
> > I will make your name great,
> > and you will be a blessing.
> > I will bless those who bless you,
> > and whoever curses you I will curse;
> > and all peoples on earth
> > will be blessed through you." (Genesis 12:1-3)

When Abraham does so and arrives in the land of Canaan, God adds this further promise, "To your offspring I will give this land" (Genesis 12:7).

This foundational promise is repeated in Genesis 15, where God undertakes a solemn oath sworn on God's own self. It is repeated again in Genesis 17, where God uses the specific language of a covenant, changes Abram's name to Abraham and Sarai's to Sarah, initiates the covenant sign of circumcision, and repeats the promise of a land for Abraham's descendants. It is repeated one more time in Genesis 22, where the promise is once again reinforced by an oath.

This repetition by itself shows how important the promise to Abraham and Sarah is, and the rest of the Bible story will confirm that. God is launching something here that will travel on through the centuries of Old Testament Israel, connect with the gospel of the kingdom of God in the preaching of Jesus and Paul, define the theology of the mission of the church in the New Testament, and ultimately come to rest only when it is completely fulfilled in the new creation. Our second of seven sentences, then, is one that spans the whole Bible story to the very end.

We need to look at this complex promise from two angles. On the one hand, it contains three *particular* promises that are the foundation of the life and faith of Israel in the Old Testament, and actually shape its core narrative. On the other hand, it envisions a *universal* goal that will embrace all nations on earth.[2]

THREE PARTICULAR PROMISES

A nation. The first thing God tells Abraham is that he will become a great nation. That sounds wonderful until you read that Sarah has not had a single child yet and Abraham is already seventy-five years old. The prospects are not very encouraging. The statistics of children born to septuagenarians in the ancient world were probably not much higher than today. I've always imagined that the angels drew in sharp whistles of breath in amazement when God announced, "I've got this great plan to save the world. It will be through that elderly, childless couple down there, by multiplying their offspring!"

Thus, right at the start of the story we find that God is going to act not merely through individuals but also through a community, a people. Of course, individuals will feature constantly in the story, for good or ill. But God's intention is to create a people, descendants of Abraham, to be the bearers of hope for the world. Whatever salvation, redemption, restoration, and blessing lie ahead will be made available for the world through this people. They are called into existence and chosen for this purpose. Eventually we will know them as Israel.

I suppose we could imagine that God might have brought salvation to the world simply by identifying individuals from all over the history and geography of the world, and then saving them individually, one by one. Of course it is true that we must all respond to God personally, one by one. But God's plan for the world (the world of Genesis 3–11 in all its personal, social, earthly, and international brokenness) has always been to create a people, a whole population ultimately for the new creation. He starts with Abraham and Sarah. And from them, eventually, God creates the people of Israel in the Old Testament. That's the first element of the promise, then—a nation to come.

Blessing. The second theme of God's promise to Abraham and Sarah is framed in the rich language of blessing. The word occurs five times in two verses. God declares

- that he will *bless* Abraham,
- that Abraham is to be a *blessing*,
- that God will *bless* those who *bless* Abraham, and
- that all families on earth will count themselves *blessed* through him.

This will be the content of the covenant relationship between God and Abraham and his people. The promise to Abraham himself is later expanded into the full covenantal affirmations that God makes to the whole people—"I will be your God and you will be my people" (occurring many times in the Old Testament). This is a relationship of mutual commitment that will bring blessing to those involved and through them will bring blessing to the world.

But what does *blessing* mean?

Well, what has the word meant so far in Genesis? The opening account of creation uses the word three times, on days five, six, and seven. Blessing is constituted by fruitfulness, abundance, and fullness in the natural order, and by humans enjoying God's own rest within God's good creation. Then, as God bids Noah set foot on the renewed world after the flood, the language overflows again—the blessing of multiplication and filling, this time embraced within God's covenant commitment to all life on earth, as we saw.

In the rest of Genesis, this same creational content of blessing occurs again and again. In fact, the Hebrew root for "bless" (*barak*) occurs eighty-eight times in Genesis, which is more than a fifth of all its usage in the whole Old Testament. When God blesses, it normally includes increase of family, or flocks, or wealth. God's blessing means enjoying the good gifts of God's creation, as God intended.

But of course we must not distort this in the way the so-called prosperity gospel does. God can and does bless people with the many forms of material blessing that are built into creation, but they are to be enjoyed *within a right relationship with God and others*. There is a relational and ethical dimension to blessing as well. It is not something mechanically doled out in exchange for tokens of faith or "seed gifts." It is not something you claim with any sense of entitlement based on the fallacious promises of greedy preachers. The rest of the Bible shows that God can bless people in many other ways, spiritually and relationally, even when they lack the fullness of the good things of God's creation.[3] We know, as Paul says, that God has blessed us with every *spiritual* blessing in Christ (Ephesians 1:3). But that wonderful truth does not eliminate the great creational dimensions of God's blessing that we enjoy simply by living in God's earth.

Land. God calls Abraham *out of* the land of Babel, the great Mesopotamian Empire. Salvation will not come to the world through human empires, however powerful. God tells Abraham to go to a land he will show him, which turns out to be the land of Canaan. Abraham himself remains a temporary resident there, moving around in a seminomadic lifestyle. At one point he buys a small plot of land to bury his wife, and that is the only foothold he has in the land God promised him. He dies without possessing the land, but with the promise of God that his descendants will do so (Hebrews 11:8-16 makes quite a point out of this life of forward-looking faith and sees in it a signpost to an even greater inheritance that lies ahead of us yet).

What is often overlooked, even though it is really quite significant, is that God himself gives the reason why the possession of the land of Canaan will not happen until several hundred years later. He tells Abraham, when he renews his promise to him in Genesis 15, that his descendants will return to this land only after four generations in slavery in a foreign land (which we later learn is Egypt), because "the sin of the Amorites has not yet reached its full measure" (Genesis 15:16). In other words, the population and culture of Canaan in Abraham's time is not yet so sinful as to justify God acting in judgment against them. But it will become so. It will reach a full measure. By the time we get to the point where Israel is poised on the edge of that land, we learn that the wickedness of the nations there has reached a depth of depravity that includes not only economic oppression, idolatry, and immoral sexual cults but even child sacrifice (Leviticus 18:1-5, 24-28; 20:22-24; Deuteronomy 9:1-6; 12:29-31). This means that, while the Israelite conquest of Canaan in the book of Joshua will always be a troublesome story, we have to see it within this moral framework of God's judgment. It cannot be seen merely as unprovoked genocide by one nation against another. It is presented as God using Israel as the agent of his justice against a sinful group of nations—in the same way as God later consistently uses other nations as the agent of his justice against Israel itself, when its sin also reaches full measure following the idolatrous ways of Canaan (some other perspectives will be offered in the next chapter).

Having said all that, however, the gift of the land to Israel is one of the core elements of God's promise to Abraham and one of the pillars of Israel's faith thereafter. They are Yahweh's people on Yahweh's land. As Yahweh's firstborn son, the land is the inheritance he has given them.

So then: people, blessing, land. Those are the substantive elements of God's promise to Abraham and Sarah:

- they will have a son, through whom God will make them into a whole nation;

- that nation will live in a covenant relationship with God; and

- they will enjoy the blessing of that relationship in the land God will give them.

ONE PARTICULAR STORY

These three great promises, however, are not just items on a list. They shape the story ahead. They give a sense of purpose and coherence to the events that follow in the rest of the Pentateuch and right on into the books of Joshua, Judges, and 1 Samuel. That long narrative, covering several centuries, is the story of God keeping his promise to Abraham, one piece at a time. Here's how.

People. The rest of the book of Genesis tells the story of how God begins to fulfill the first element in the promise, though with a great deal of suspense as to whether and when he ever will. Years go by before Isaac is born. Then God instructs Abraham to sacrifice him. Isaac is spared that fate, but his family is then split by sibling rivalry and death threats between Esau and Jacob. They are reconciled, but then Jacob's own family falls into more prolonged feuding over Joseph, who ends up in Egypt and by God's grace saves the whole family from starvation and extinction. Yet more reconciliation of brothers is needed. By the end of Genesis, Abraham's family has grown to seventy people living as famine refugees in Egypt.

Hardly yet a great nation. But it's a start.

Blessing. The story of how God brings Israel into covenant relationship with himself occupies the next two and a half books—Exodus, Leviticus, and the first part of Numbers. Israel has become a great nation (Exodus 1:7)—that much is fulfilled. But they are in slavery. God acts to redeem them out of Egypt and then brings them to himself at Mount Sinai. There God enters into a covenant relationship with them and calls them to love and obey him as the way of enjoying the blessings of their redemption (note that salvation comes before law; we'll come back to that point in the next chapter). Even this part of the story involves suspense too, as Israel breaks the covenant just as soon as it has been made (Exodus 32–34). By God's forgiving grace, they are saved from destruction, and God gives them a system of sacrifice and priesthood, and a place where his presence will dwell among them (the tabernacle) so that the covenant relationship can be maintained into the future. Leviticus ends with a promise of ongoing covenant blessing (or the opposite, if the people persist in sinful rebellion).

The relationship is established—not without serious obstacles, but on the basis of God's forgiving and sustaining grace.

Land. All of the events and teaching between Exodus 19 and Numbers 9 take place at Mount Sinai. In Numbers 10, however, God tells the Israelites to move forward and go up into the Promised Land—the third element in his promise to Abraham and Sarah. Once again (we're getting used to this), the narrative is threatened with suspense and failure. The Israelites chicken out. The people whom God has rescued from Egypt refuse to go on into the land (Numbers 13–14), and as a result they end up spending that whole generation (another thirty-eight years) in the wilderness. The story seems to have stalled once more. However, eventually the next generation reach the borders of the land, camped in Moab on the eastern side of the River Jordan. There Moses gives his final speeches of warning, encouragement, and instruction, as presented in the book of Deuteronomy. The whole book is oriented toward the land ahead, and it is repeatedly described as the land that God promised to their ancestors. Deuteronomy ends, however, with the people still not in the land, but on the point of moving in.

In a sense the Pentateuch ends with the promise of God behind them and the future of God's promise still ahead of them, which is where the people of God always stand. Eventually it is Joshua who takes Israel into the land. Once again the story immediately breaks up into the fracturing of the Israelite tribes, during the era described in the book of Judges. Finally, it is David who brings unity to the tribes (though it will only last one more generation) and gives Israel effective possession and control of the whole land of promise.

We can see that these three elements of God's promise to Abraham and Sarah run like a sequence of themes through the long and complex narratives from Genesis to 1 Samuel, keeping the story moving in a direction already set at the start. It is one story, fulfilling one promise in three parts.

One Universal Goal

We must not leave out the last thing that God promised Abraham, the one expressed in the theme sentence for this chapter: "All peoples on earth will be blessed through you" (Genesis 12:3). This is the bottom line, not only in the sense that it is the conclusion and climax of the whole speech but also as the purpose and goal of all that has gone before. God is speaking to Abraham, but God's eyes are on the rest of the world. God is promising to make one great nation out of Abraham's descendants, but his ultimate purpose is to bring blessing to all nations on earth. The verse is very particular ("through you"), but its goal is dramatically universal ("all peoples on earth").

This is the sentence that is like a trigger for the rest of the Bible's story. As such, it is truly astonishing. Here is God talking to one old man with an elderly wife who has been unable to have any children, and God tells him that he will be the means of God's bringing blessing to all the families of nations in the world. We must not think of that last line as merely an afterthought, as if God means, "Oh and by the way, a few other folks will get blessed too." On the contrary, this specific part of the promise is highlighted by repetition. It comes five times altogether in Genesis (Genesis 12:3; 18:18; 22:18 [all three to Abraham]; 26:4-5 [to Isaac]; 28:14 [to Jacob]). It is foundational to the whole story to come.

In fact, what we have here in Genesis 12:1-3 is the launch of God's *redemptive* mission. This is the opening act of God's great mission to restore what humanity seemed intent on wrecking and to save humanity itself from the consequences of our own wicked folly. In other words, this is the start of salvation history. But it is expressed in terms of *blessing.* As we've seen, the repeated use of this word *blessing* links the story of Abraham with the creation narratives that precede it. God's work of redemption will take place within and for the benefit of both the created order and the nations of humanity.

A global gospel. "All nations," says God. This is good news, surely. In the world of fractured nations, climaxing in Genesis

11, God promises to bring blessing that will reach to the same extent. There is a great trajectory from the tribes, languages, and nations of Genesis 10, who stand in need of redemption, healing, and blessing, to that "great multitude that no one could count, from every nation, tribe, people and language," who will constitute the redeemed humanity in the new creation (Revelation 7:9). The Abrahamic covenant is thus one of the key unifying threads in the whole Bible.

It is true that Israel in the Old Testament often seems to forget the reason for its existence—to be this people of Abraham for the sake of the blessing of the rest of the nations. They succumb to the same kind of ethnocentric hostility to outsiders that afflicts most nations. However, *in their worship* this note of the universal purpose of God for all nations often shines through. Worship calls for faith and imagination, such as we find in songs like this:

All the ends of the earth
    will remember and turn to the Lord,
and all the families of the nations
    will bow down before him. (Psalm 22:27)

The nobles of the nations assemble
    as the people of the God of Abraham,
for the kings of the earth belong to God;
    he is greatly exalted. (Psalm 47:9)

All the nations you have made
    will come and worship before you, Lord;
    they will bring glory to your name. (Psalm 86:9)[4]

Do you ever wonder (as I often do) how the average Israelite singing such songs envisaged such vast worldwide horizons? Yet they sang them. These songs speak the truth of Israel's gospel, announced in advance to Abraham—the good news of God's covenant commitment to bless all nations on earth.

It is no wonder, then, that the apostle Paul calls this verse, Genesis 12:3, quite simply "the gospel in advance" (Galatians 3:8). The good news, announced to Abraham and ultimately fulfilled in Christ, is that God's great plan is the blessing of all nations. In the context of Galatians, of course, that gospel for all nations includes the Gentiles, which made it controversial among Paul's own fellow Jews. Paul's grasp of the significance of Abraham is set out even more fully in Romans 3:28–4:25. Paul sees clearly that bringing Gentiles into the covenant family of God is not *contrary* to the Scriptures (as his opponents say) but rather *the fulfillment* of the Scriptures—that is, what God has always planned to do, according to his promise to Abraham.

It is important to understand that Paul is not just using Abraham as an *illustration* of the gospel or of his teaching about justification by grace through faith. No, Abraham is the *beginning* of the gospel. The God of Abraham declares that through the people of Israel (as they will come to be known) God will deal with the problem caused by human sin and divine curse (the problem so clearly laid out in Genesis 3–11). What God accomplishes through the life, death, and resurrection of Jesus is the center point of the story of what God promised to Abraham. When that great multitude from all nations is gathered as the population of the new creation, God will declare that promise finally fulfilled. As Richard Bauckham writes,

> The ultimate goal of God's promise to Abraham is that blessing will prevail over curse. It does so when the seed of Abraham, the singled-out descendant of Abraham, the Messiah, becomes "a curse for us . . . so that in Christ Jesus the blessing of Abraham might come to the Gentiles" (Galatians 3:13-14). It is in this light that Paul can call the promise to Abraham that the nations will be blessed the gospel. . . .

The gospel is that in Christ Jesus the curse has been set aside and God's creative purpose for the blessing of his creation is established beyond any possibility of reversal.[5]

A chosen people. "Through you," God says also. The global goal of blessing for all nations is to be accomplished through the particular means of *this* people, the people descended from Abraham, the Old Testament people of Israel. They, Israel, are chosen for this purpose.

The connection between the choice of Israel (in Abraham) and the promise to bless all the nations on earth is very clearly expressed in Genesis 18:18-19. God is speaking to himself, after his meal with Abraham and Sarah, and says, "Abraham will surely become a great and powerful nation, and all nations on earth will be blessed through him. For I have chosen him, so that he will direct his children and his household after him to keep the way of the LORD by doing what is right and just, so that the Lord will bring about for Abraham what he has promised him" (Genesis 18:18-19).

This makes two things clear. First, the election of Israel was not a *rejection* of all the other nations but precisely for their benefit. We should not think of our doctrine of election as only about who gets to be saved. The first time we see it clearly in the Bible—in God's election of Abraham—it is in the context of God's *mission*. God's *plan* is to bless all nations; God's *means* is to use this particular nation. Being a chosen people is not an exclusive privilege; it is, rather, a massive responsibility.

Second, that responsibility is ethical. God wants Israel to be a people who will be taught to live distinctively from the surrounding nations. The context of those verses in Genesis 18 is the impending judgment of God on Sodom and Gomorrah. In that world (which is still our world), God chooses Abraham to create a people of contrast, a people who will walk in the way of the Lord, not the way of Sodom, who will do righteousness and justice, not cruelty and oppression.

The rest of the Old Testament shows how God, through the law and the prophets, keeps calling Israel back to that high commitment—to be "a light to the nations"—and how Israel repeatedly fails. God's purpose, however, does not fail. For it will indeed be as the God of Israel and through the Messiah of Israel that God will accomplish the purpose of their election—opening up the blessing of the gospel to all nations through the Lord Jesus Christ.

- three -

EXODUS

*I am the L*ORD *your God, who brought you
out of Egypt, out of the land of slavery.*

EXODUS 20:2

Q. When is the first not the beginning?

A. When it's the first commandment.

For, indeed, the first commandment is not the beginning of the Ten Commandments, or the Decalogue, as it is called. That famous text begins not with a command but with our third sentence, this great affirmation: "I am the LORD your God, who brought you out of Egypt, out of the land of slavery" (Exodus 20:2).

That statement conveniently summarizes the story so far and presents it as the foundation for all that will follow. It is *the* story of redemption in the Old Testament, which shapes Israel's concept of God as Redeemer and provides believers in both Old and New Testaments with their template for what redemption means. It is the statement that stands at the head of the section of the Old Testament known as the law.

In this chapter we will learn the story of redemption (the exodus), followed by the giving of God's law and the making of the covenant. It is important to hold all these together and understand them in relation to God's long-term mission to bless the nations, as we saw in chapter two.

God's Redemption

The story of redemption unfolds dramatically in Exodus 1–18. Genesis ends with the sons of Jacob having arrived in Egypt as refugees from famine, being welcomed there by Pharaoh and reconciled with their brother Joseph, whom they sold into slavery in Egypt decades earlier. Exodus opens by telling us that the family (seventy persons in all) not only survived but also manifestly thrived and multiplied extraordinarily in Egypt. But then a change in the government of Egypt brings a change in the state's policy toward this immigrant ethnic minority of Hebrews in their midst. The government launches a fear-based policy of oppression that includes forced labor in construction and agricultural projects combined with a murderous attempt at population control. The children of Israel (as they are now called), endure every kind of bondage—economic, political, social, and spiritual—and cry out in their suffering.

A boy is born to Hebrew parents and, by the actions of his cunning mother and watchful sister, escapes the Pharaoh's command that newborn boys should be drowned in the Nile. Rescued by Pharaoh's own daughter, he is named Moses and grows up in the Egyptian court. After an abortive attempt to exercise violent justice on behalf of one of his own people, he flees into exile from Egypt to Midian, where he finds asylum, a wife, and a job in the shepherding household of Jethro, the priest of Midian.

God called Abraham at the age of seventy-five. Now, with the same disregard for the alleged vigor of youth, God calls Moses at the age of eighty. Moses has a surprising encounter with the living God, who appears in the flames of a bush that is burning but not consumed. God identifies himself as the God of Abraham, Isaac, and Jacob; declares that he has seen and heard the desperate plight of their descendants in Egypt and is intent on delivering them from their bondage; and commissions Moses to go down and do the job. Moses' protests are overcome by God's revelation of the name by which God chooses to be known from then on—Yahweh—and the promise of God's constant presence. Two octogenarians—Moses and his brother Aaron, three years older than himself—head down to confront the might of the Egyptian Empire.

The government of Egypt, in the person of the Pharaoh (who is never named), is reluctant to lose the economic benefit of its enslaved workforce and refuses even more strongly to recognize the name or authority of this God Yahweh whom Moses claims to represent. Egypt rejects Moses' request to let the Hebrews go. A massive conflict then takes place: God sends on Egypt a sequence of plagues, relatively mild at first but increasing in severity, accompanied by repeated demands to let the people go. Egypt has the opportunity to change course, but each time there is an increasing hardening of Pharaoh's heart against the manifest power of Yahweh and the appeals of Moses and even of his own officials. Finally, when the tenth plague strikes down the firstborn of all Egyptian households, including Pharaoh's, Pharaoh implores Moses to get his people out that very night, which he does—only for Pharaoh to change his mind yet again and pursue them, trapping them on the shore of the Sea of Reeds. Then comes the greatest miracle of all, remembered through all Israel's generations to the present day.

By the power of the wind at God's command, the sea parts to allow the Israelites to escape on dry land but returns to drown the pursuing Egyptian army. The deliverance of Israel is complete. This is the night and day of their redemption.

Redemption. That is the word God uses when he promises in advance what he is about to do.

> "Therefore, say to the Israelites: 'I am the Lord, and I will bring you out from under the yoke of the Egyptians. I will free you from being slaves to them, and *I will redeem you* with an outstretched arm and with mighty acts of judgment. I will take you as my own people, and I will be your God. Then you will know that I am the Lord your God, who brought you out from under the yoke of the Egyptians. And I will bring you to the land I swore with uplifted hand to give to Abraham, to Isaac and to Jacob. I will give it to you as a possession. I am the Lord.'" (Exodus 6:6-8; my italics)

Redemption is the word that Moses and Miriam use when they celebrate the deliverance at the sea:

> Who among the gods
>   is like you, Lord?
> Who is like you—
>   majestic in holiness,
> awesome in glory,
>   working wonders?
>
> You stretch out your right hand,
>   and the earth swallows your enemies.
> In your unfailing love you will lead
>   *the people you have redeemed.*
> In your strength you will guide them
>   to your holy dwelling. (Exodus 15:11-13; my italics)

And *redemption* is the word that is in the background, even if not actually used, in our key sentence: "I am the Lord your God, who brought you out of Egypt, out of the land of slavery" (Exodus 20:2). It is only three months after that miraculous deliverance from Egypt that the Israelites arrive at Mount Sinai, so the memory of their redemption is very fresh. God intends that they should always remember that it was Yahweh, the living God, who accomplished their salvation. Every time an Israelite father teaches the essence of God's law to his family, in the form of the Ten Commandments, he must begin with that statement about who their God is and what he has done for them, the story of their nation's redemption. If further questions are asked, he must tell the story even more fully:

> In the future, when your son asks you, "What is the meaning of the stipulations, decrees and laws the LORD our God has commanded you?" tell him: "We were slaves of Pharaoh in Egypt, but the LORD brought us out of Egypt with a mighty hand. Before our eyes the LORD sent signs and wonders—great and terrible—on Egypt and Pharaoh and his whole household. But he brought us out from there to bring us in and give us the land he promised on oath to our ancestors. The LORD commanded us to obey all these decrees and to fear the LORD our God, so that we might always prosper and be kept alive, as is the case today." (Deuteronomy 6:20-24)

Thus before we turn to the Ten Commandments and the rest of Israel's law, we need to do what they did—that is, we must first look back and remember that story of redemption, the story of Exodus 1–18, summarized above. But then we must also look forward to what lies ahead in the purposes of God.

GOD'S INTENTION

Why does God choose to rescue this people out of slavery? Why did he act with such determined justice against Pharaoh's murderous and unrepentant oppression? Does the text give us any insight into God's motives and God's intentions? Yes, we can see three quite clearly.

This text gives us the first two factors that motivate God to act. "The Israelites groaned in their slavery and cried out, and their cry for help because of their slavery went up to God. God heard their groaning and he remembered his covenant with Abraham, with Isaac and with Jacob. So God looked on the Israelites and was concerned about them" (Exodus 2:23-25; see also Exodus 3:7-10, 16-17; 4:29-31).

The first factor is that God "remembered his covenant with Abraham." This does not mean that God has forgotten it, but simply that God decides it is now time to act on it and keep the promise he made to Abraham in Genesis 15:13-16 that he would bring Abraham's descendants back out of their slavery in a foreign land.

The second factor is God's compassion for their suffering. This is mentioned several times. God sees their plight and hears their cry and "was concerned about them." God responds with compassion to human suffering and anger when human injustice causes it.

In relation to Israel's situation in Egypt, these two motivating factors arise from the distant *past* (God's faithfulness to his covenant promise to Abraham) and from the immediate *present* (God's justice, manifested in compassion for the oppressed and judgment against the oppressor).

The third motivating factor is expressed when God finally gets the Israelites to himself at Mount Sinai. It involves God's intentions for Israel as a nation, within his long-term *future* vision for all nations and the whole earth. God has redeemed Israel because God has a mission for the whole world. That's what becomes clear in God's opening speech at Mount Sinai (Exodus 19:3-6).

Notice how these words of God also refer to the *past*, have a vision for the *future*, and call for a response in the *present*:

Then Moses went up to God, and the LORD called to him from the mountain and said, "This is what you are to say to the descendants of Jacob and what you are to tell the people of Israel: 'You yourselves have seen what I did to Egypt, and how I carried you on eagles' wings and brought you to myself. Now if you obey me fully and keep my covenant, then out of all nations you will be my treasured possession. Although the whole earth is mine, you will be for me a kingdom of priests and a holy nation.' These are the words you are to speak to the Israelites." (Exodus 19:3-6)

The first thing God does is to remind the people of God's own initiative of saving grace—"You yourselves have seen what *I* did" (Exodus 19:4). They certainly have. Three months earlier they were being whipped and beaten as slaves, their sons murdered, their lives unbearable. Now they are liberated from all that. God says, I did that. Whatever future lies ahead, and whatever demands God might make of them—it will all be *in response* to what God has already accomplished for them. Redemption leads to responsibility.

Then God spells out Israel's identity and role, in phrases that combine the universal and the particular, in the same way as characterized God's promise to Abraham, as we saw in the last chapter.

On the one hand (the universal perspective), God's view from the top of Mount Sinai, as it were, is globally embracing. He is the God of "the whole earth" and of "all nations" (Exodus 19:5-6). These are strongly Abrahamic words, and they remind us that this is the same God who has introduced himself to Moses as "the God of Abraham" (Exodus 3:6). God has just rescued *one* nation out of slavery, but his goal (as promised to Abraham) is ultimately that *all* nations will enjoy the blessing of God's redeeming grace. God has just demonstrated his power in one land (Egypt), but his goal is that his name should be known in *all* the earth (Exodus 9:16).

On the other hand (the particular perspective), God holds out to Israel the prospect of a unique relationship with God ("my treasured possession") and a unique role on God's behalf in the midst of the nations ("you will be for me a kingdom of priests and a holy nation"). Priests in Israel are middlemen. They stand in between God and the rest of the people, operating in both directions. They are teachers of God's law (Leviticus 10:11; Deuteronomy 33:10; Jeremiah 18:18; Malachi 2:7). Through the priests God will become known to the people. They bring the sacrifices of the people to God, declaring to those who bring them that ritual uncleanness is cleansed, or sins atoned for, so that they can come back into joyful fellowship with God and his people. Through the priests people can come to God. Priests bring God to the people and bring people to God. In that double role, they *bless* the people (Numbers 6:22-27).

Thus, when God says that Israel is to be his priesthood in the midst of the nations, he means (among other things) that they will be for him to the rest of the nations what their priests are to them. Israel will be the people through whom God will make himself known to the world (as he has done through the Scriptures of Israel that we now call the Old Testament), and they will be the people through whom God will draw the world to himself (as he continues to do through the Messiah of Israel, our Lord Jesus Christ). This definitive statement of Israel's identity and role draws them as a people into the mission of God for the world, to be the vehicle of God's blessing to the nations.

In order to fulfill such a missional role among the nations, Israel must be "a holy nation"—that is, different and distinctive from surrounding peoples, not merely in religious practice but in every aspect of their social, economic, and political lives. That indeed will be the purpose of the law God will give them, to which we'll turn in a moment.

How can Israel ever fit such a role or fulfill such a responsibility? That is where the conditional clause at the beginning of Exodus 19:5 is so important: "If you obey me fully and keep my covenant, then . . ." God's intention is that Israel should be the people through whom God will accomplish his mission for all nations. That intention requires a people who will live and walk in God's ways (as God said to Abraham in Genesis 18:18-19).

Crucially, however, we must take note that this requirement (that Israel should obey God's law and covenant) is *not* a condition of salvation. God has already saved them and now calls for their response to that historic grace. But it *is* a condition of their mission. God does not say, "If you obey me, then I will save you." Rather, he says, "Now that I have saved you, if you will obey me, then you can *be* something for me in the world. Here is your mission, should you choose to accept it." Which they do (three times, in fact; Exodus 19:8; 24:3, 7) but still fail to live up to.

God's Covenant

We can see that this whole arrangement between God and Israel is relational and mutual. Something is affirmed and promised involving both parties in a committed relationship. That is the very nature of biblical covenants—and particularly this covenant, between God and Old Testament Israel.

Already we have seen two major covenants in the Old Testament story. First, God's covenant with Noah—God's committed promise to all life on earth. There is a covenantal relationship between God and creation. Then, second, God's covenant with Abraham, that he will become a great nation, that they will enjoy God's blessing and live in God's land, and that through them all nations on earth will come to know God's blessing. Now, third, we have the Sinai covenant, made with Israel through Moses. However, in fact this is not a new covenant but a development of the covenant with Abraham, now that his descendants have actually become the nation God promised. Here is how God explains it just before the exodus:

> I have heard the groaning of the Israelites, whom the Egyptians are enslaving, and I have remembered my covenant [i.e., the covenant with Abraham, Isaac, and Jacob].
>
> Therefore, say to the Israelites: "I am the LORD, and I will bring you out from under the yoke of the Egyptians. I will free you from being slaves to them, and I will redeem you with an outstretched arm and with mighty acts of judgment. I will take you as my own people, and I will be your God. Then you will know that I am the LORD your God, who brought you out from under the yoke of the Egyptians. And I will bring you to the land I swore with uplifted hand to give to Abraham, to Isaac and to Jacob. I will give it to you as a possession. I am the LORD." (Exodus 6:5-8)

The heartbeat of that relationship is stated in Exodus 6:7: "I will take you as my own people, and I will be your God." That mutual commitment of God to Israel and Israel to God is the essence of the covenant. On Israel's side it requires committed obedience to Yahweh as their covenant Lord. The covenant, then, is both a solemn and formal promise, and a strong and binding commitment.

In Exodus 24 we have the account of the day the covenant at Sinai is sealed. Here is the central section. Notice the combination of sacrifices, with the blood sprinkled both on the altar (representing God) and on the people, along with the double commitment by the people to obey God's word:

> When Moses went and told the people all the LORD's words and laws, they responded with one voice, "Everything the LORD has said we will do." Moses then wrote down everything the LORD had said.

He got up early the next morning and built an altar at the foot of the mountain and set up twelve stone pillars representing the twelve tribes of Israel. Then he sent young Israelite men, and they offered burnt offerings and sacrificed young bulls as fellowship offerings to the LORD. Moses took half of the blood and put it in bowls, and the other half he splashed against the altar. Then he took the Book of the Covenant and read it to the people. They responded, "We will do everything the LORD has said; we will obey."

Moses then took the blood, sprinkled it on the people and said, "This is the blood of the covenant that the LORD has made with you in accordance with all these words." (Exodus 24:3-8)

A generation later, Moses renews the covenant before the Israelites cross over the River Jordan into the Promised Land. Here is how he expresses that relationship, in two classic balancing verses. "You have declared this day that the LORD is your God and that you will walk in obedience to him, that you will keep his decrees, commands and laws—that you will listen to him. And the LORD has declared this day that you are his people, his treasured possession as he promised, and that you are to keep all his commands" (Deuteronomy 26:17-18).

GOD'S LAW

We come, then, to the law itself, beginning with those Ten Commandments that we have now set in the context of the story so far, God's redemption and God's intention.

Defining the terms. We speak of Old Testament law, but it's not always clear what we are talking about.[1] For Israelites (and for Jews today), the word was Torah. As I pointed out at the start of chapter one, that was the title for the first five books of the

DEUTERONOMY AS AN ANCIENT NEAR EASTERN TREATY

The book of Deuteronomy is the clearest whole articulation of the covenant relationship. The structure of its content is very similar to the structure of international treaties from that period in the ancient Near East. The Hittite Empire, for example, typically made treaties between the Hittite great king and the nations that were subject to him. Several such ancient treaty documents have been discovered, and they take a standard form—a form that is reflected in Deuteronomy. Here are six typical elements in those treaty documents that are reflected in the shape of Deuteronomy.

- Identification of the great king (Yahweh as Israel's sovereign Lord; e.g., Deuteronomy 5:6; 6:4)

- The history of the relationship (what Yahweh has done for Israel; Deuteronomy 1–3)

- General requirements (a broad call for loyalty; Deuteronomy 4–11)

- Specific stipulations (more detailed laws; Deuteronomy 12–26)

- Blessings and curses (for loyal obedience to the great king, or for rebellion and disobedience, respectively; Deuteronomy 27–28)

- Witnesses and reading of the documents (Deuteronomy 29–31)

This suggests that the Israelites, perhaps Moses himself, found this political structure to be a useful metaphor through which to understand the relationship between Yahweh (as the Great King) and his people. It also helps to explain why, in later centuries, when Israel does in fact fall into such sin and disobedience against God, the prophets interpret that failure as rebellion and disloyalty to the Great King. The Israelites are breaking the terms of the covenant and thereby incurring the threats and sanctions that were built into it from the start.

Bible—the whole Pentateuch, from Genesis to Deuteronomy. But Torah does not just mean "law" in our sense of statutes or legislation. It means "teaching" or "guidance." The Torah provides that teaching by means of its great narrative from creation to the borders of the Promised Land, as well as by the sections that are laws in our sense of the word.

However, within the Torah come several sections that are more explicitly laws—commandments, instructions, cases, penalties, and so on. Here are the main ones.

The Decalogue (Exodus 20:2-17; Deuteronomy 5:6-21). This list of ten commandments holds a special place, as having been spoken and written directly by God. They form a summary of the essential principles and boundaries of the rest of the more detailed laws. It is a remarkably comprehensive list. At the same time, its brevity aids memorization, so that the core stipulations of covenant membership could be clearly known. Break these commands, and you step outside the sphere of covenant relationship, responsibility, and blessing. The order of the list also illustrates the vertical and horizontal dimensions of the covenant relationship—that is, our relationship with God and our relationship with other people. The first four commandments are primarily vertical, though the fourth (the Sabbath command) is also for human benefit, while the second six are horizontal. The two dimensions are really inseparable, as Jesus points out in combining love for God and love for our neighbor as the two greatest commandments in the law.

The Book of the Covenant (Exodus 20:22–23:33). This term is used in Exodus 24:7 to describe the short body of laws that immediately follows the Decalogue in the context of the covenant ceremony at Mount Sinai. The laws in these chapters are mostly case laws—describing typical situations of dispute, damage, assault, negligence, accident, and so on, and prescribing the kind of compensatory actions to be taken. Such laws, like precedents in contemporary legal systems, generated principles by which other cases could be judged. In other words, this is not a complete book of laws to govern everything that might ever happen, but rather a list of guidelines and examples that shape and inform the way local judges will deal with issues as they arose. There is a strong concern for the needs of the vulnerable in society and for the integrity of the whole judicial system.

Leviticus. The whole book, apart from a few narrative passages of events at Mount Sinai, is taken up with regulations for the system of sacrifices, the multiple and varied duties of priests, the symbolic distinctions of clean and unclean foods, and then a number of social, familial, sexual, and economic laws that promote Israel's distinctiveness (holiness) as the people of Yahweh.

Deuteronomy's collection (Deuteronomy 4–26). The word *Deuteronomy* literally means "second law," but it isn't really. It is, rather, a *renewing* of the covenant and a preaching of the law to the second generation after the exodus, as they are camped in Moab on the border of the Promised Land. The book presents itself as the speeches of Moses shortly before his death, urging the Israelites to move forward with Yahweh their God, to stay loyal to him in the midst of the challenges of Canaanite idolatry that lie ahead, and to organize their society in the land according to the constitution and laws God gave them at Sinai. The book begins with historical memory and ends with future anticipation of what lies ahead. In between, in Deuteronomy 4–26, there is a whole section of laws for life in the land, many of which are repetitions of the same laws in Exodus or Leviticus but with added explanation and motivation.

Celebrating grace. If we want to understand Old Testament law, we need to start by thinking of it in the way the Old Testament Israelites themselves did. Some people have a very negative view of Old Testament law because they approach it entirely through some of the things the apostle Paul writes about it. We must remember that Paul was engaged in a heated controversy with some Jewish leaders (many of them Pharisees like Paul himself) who had turned the law into something it was never intended to be—a kind of badge or guarantee of righteous standing with God, of belonging to the right people. They were insisting that Gentiles who had come to faith in Messiah Jesus as their Lord and Savior must also become Jewish converts (proselytes), by being circumcised and fully observing the Old Testament law. They insisted that keeping the laws of the Torah was a necessary condition of belonging to God's people, rather than faith in Christ and in the grace and promises of God. Paul opposed them for distorting the Scriptures. Their view of the law was not what the Old Testament actually teaches.

The law is not a burden imposed by God as a condition of righteousness and salvation. The law is the gift of God to people *already redeemed*, in order to enable them to go on living within the sphere of his blessing. It is given on the foundation of God's grace that has been demonstrated in the redemption already accomplished (see above), and it is given in order to help them respond appropriately and live in the way God wants. Devout and godly Israelites *celebrate* the law as something good and positive, something sweet and precious, something to delight in and be nourished by. Here is what some of the psalmists think about God's law. It is clear they do not see it as a gloomy dead weight of legalistic rules. They appreciate and value it highly.

> The law of the LORD is perfect,
> > refreshing the soul.
> The statues of the LORD are trustworthy,
> > making wise the simple.

The precepts of the LORD are right,
	giving joy to the heart.
The commands of the LORD are radiant,
	giving light to the eyes.
The fear of the LORD is pure,
	enduring forever.
The ordinances of the LORD are firm,
	and all of them are righteous.

They are more precious than gold,
	than much pure gold;
They are sweeter than honey,
	than honey from the comb. (Psalm 19:7-10)

I will walk about in freedom,
	for I have sought out your precepts. . . .
I delight in your commands,
	because I love them. . . .
Oh, how I love your law! . . .
I love your commands more than gold,
	more than pure gold.
	(Psalm 119:45, 47, 97, 127)

This is why our sentence is so important. We should not read the Ten Commandments or the rest of Old Testament law without that opening reminder of the story of salvation in which they are set. God's law is a gift of God's grace to people who have already experienced the grace of God's redeeming love and power. It is something to be celebrated with gratitude.

Shaping for mission. We should read God's law, however, not only looking back to the story so far but also looking forward to the story to come. God gives this law to this people *for a purpose*, for a purpose that is consistent with why God created them in the first place. Remember God's promise to Abraham, Isaac, and

Jacob? "Through your offspring all nations on earth will be blessed." God's mission, through Israel, is to bless all nations. Israel's mission, therefore, is to *be* the people of God and to serve his purpose in the world. For that purpose, they need to shape up, to live as a community that reflects the character and ways of the living God, in a world full of the false gods and idols that fallen humanity manufactures in our own sinful likeness. Israel is to be different from the nations in order to be a light to the nations. As we saw a moment ago, from Exodus 19:5-6, that is the whole point of being a "holy nation" in the midst of "all nations," and the reason why they need to obey God's law and keep his covenant.

This missional motivation for keeping God's law is expressed in Deuteronomy. God envisages a people who, by living as a society governed by God's values and standards, will become a visible model to the nations, bearing witness to the presence of the God they worship by the admirable quality of their whole social system:

> See, I have taught you decrees and laws as the LORD my God commanded me, so that you may follow them in the land you are entering to take possession of it. Observe them carefully, for this will show your wisdom and understanding to the nations, who will hear about all these decrees and say, "Surely this great nation is a wise and understanding people." What other nation is so great as to have their gods near them the way the LORD our God is near us whenever we pray to him? And what other nation is so great as to have such righteous decrees and laws as this body of laws I am setting before you today? (Deuteronomy 4:5-8)

If God's people live in God's way, then other people should notice and ask questions. We are meant to be a living advertisement for the God we worship by the quality of the way we live. That principle is built into Israel's law and is echoed by Jesus and the teaching of the apostles in the New Testament.

Reflecting God. One of the commonest ways that the Old Testament speaks about obeying God's law is to "walk in the ways of the Lord." That means not only to do what God says but also to follow God's example—to follow in his footsteps, as it were. How do the Israelites know what their God Yahweh is like? By remembering what he has done. As we saw above, the exodus was the massive demonstration of the character of God—his love, compassion, faithfulness, and justice. *If that is what God is like for Israel, that is what the Israelites must be like to one another and others.*

Frequently, in the law codes of the Old Testament, you'll find that the exodus is referred to by way of reminder. God says, "This is what I did for you; now here is what I want you to do for others." (Does that sound like somebody else you may have heard of? "Do unto others what you would like others to do for you," or "Love your enemies . . . that you may be children of your Father in heaven. He causes the sun to rise on the evil and the good, and sends the rain on the righteous and the unrighteous" [Matthew 5:44-45]—i.e., be like him.) Here's a typical example. When an Israelite householder releases a Hebrew slave under the statutory six-year release law, he is to give the slave a generous redundancy package of grain, animals, and wine to see him on his way. Why should he do that? Here's the instruction, and the reason for it: "And when you release them, do not send them away empty-handed. Supply them liberally from your flock, your threshing floor and your winepress. Give to them as the Lord your God has blessed you. Remember that you were slaves in Egypt and the Lord your God redeemed you. *That is why I give you this command today*" (Deuteronomy 15:13-15; my italics).

Other examples include Exodus 23:9; Leviticus 19:33-36; 25:42-43; Deuteronomy 24:17-22.

Moses stresses that Israel is not only to imitate what God had done for them but also simply to reflect the character of God as they see it in action:

> To the LORD your God belong the heavens, even the highest heavens, the earth and everything in it. . . . The LORD your God is God of gods and Lord of lords, the great God, mighty and awesome, who shows no partiality and accepts no bribes. He defends the cause of the fatherless and the widow, and loves the foreigner residing among you, giving them food and clothing. (Deuteronomy 10:14, 17-18)

Here is this great God who owns and rules the universe, and who is the God of utter integrity in whom is no corruption. But where will you find this God in action? Where you might least expect: among the poor and needy, the family-less, the land-less, the home-less. Those are the ones Yahweh God cares for and provides for. Since that is what God is like, then the logic is obvious, and Moses states it in the very next verse: "And you are to love those who are foreigners, for you yourselves were foreigners in Egypt" (Deuteronomy 10:19). That is what the imitation and reflection of God looks like—doing what God wants to be done, acting in the world as God would act. It is a powerful principle, reflected in the teaching of Jesus himself. God's law is given to help God's people reflect God's character.

Anticipating failure. But this all sounds very idealistic, you may be thinking. We know that the Old Testament Israelites never live up to such standards. Indeed we do, and the Old Testament itself tells us so very clearly. But here's the thing. God knows that too perfectly well and tells them so long in advance. Israel's failure is no surprise to God. In fact, the law itself *anticipates* Israel's failure and provides a remedy for it—a double remedy. On the one hand, there is the system of sacrifices described in Leviticus 1–7 (which we will briefly outline in the next chapter). These deal with what might be called routine sins and ritual uncleanness. These sacrifices cannot ultimately take away high-handed sin (sinning defiantly; see Numbers 15:30-31). For that the only answer is to turn in repentance to God and trust in his grace—as Psalm 51 puts it (see especially Psalm 51:16-17). On the other hand, God assures Israel that by his own power and grace, even after the outworking of his judgment, God will restore those who turn back to him. This is the pattern (sin, judgment, grace, restoration) that is laid out in Deuteronomy 29–30. Those chapters could be summarized like this:

- God reminds Israel again that he has redeemed them from slavery and made them his covenant people.

- God has given them his law, to equip them live in the way that will be good for them and bring them blessing. They have made their covenant commitment to love and obey God in return.

- *However*, God knows very well that the Israelites will *not* keep this law. They have shown how rebellious and sinful they were even while Moses was alive. As the generations go by after his death, they will become even worse.

- Thus, God will have to bring down on them all the threats and warnings that are built into this covenant. Because Israel will persistently break God's covenant, they will experience the curses of the covenant, not its blessing.

- God's judgment will fall, through the attacks of their enemies, and they will be driven out of their land and scattered among foreign nations.

• *However*, God assures them, right here in Deuteronomy before all this happens, that judgment does not have to be God's final word or Israel's final condition. There can be hope beyond judgment. Yahweh will still be the God of grace, love, and forgiveness. God will *enable* them to seek him with all their heart and soul, to love him and obey him. So turn back to God. Choose life, not death.

The law itself (in Deuteronomy) anticipates the future failure of Israel. Indeed, these chapters of Deuteronomy not only give us a clear theology of sin, judgment, repentance, grace, and restoration; but they also give us the history of Israel in advance. This is the story of the Old Testament.

When we turn back to the apostle Paul, we are not surprised (any more than God was) that the law in itself could not make sinners and rebels good and perfect. But the fault is not in the law but in the people. That's why Paul talks about the law being "powerless . . . because it was weakened by the flesh," meaning our sinful human nature (Romans 8:3). That's why the Israelites find that the law brings them death. It exposes their sin. It brings them under God's curse and judgment. But here's the key point: *This is not some new discovery by Paul. The law itself says as much.* The law calls for Israel's faithfulness; but the law also expected Israel's failure. It is realistic. But then the law also points beyond judgment to *future hope* in the saving and restoring grace of God. It points, in other words, ultimately to the Lord Jesus Christ, as Paul sees so clearly.

four

DAVID

The LORD has sought out a man after his own heart and appointed him ruler of his people.

1 SAMUEL 13:14

The apostle Paul, I reckon, would have been far better at this "Old Testament in seven sentences" job than I am. He just about managed it in a sermon in a Jewish synagogue in Pisidian Antioch. Doubtless it's a bit abbreviated from what Paul may have expanded on, but even so it's impressively condensed. A wave of the hand, a call for attention, and he's off. He gets from Abraham to Jesus, if not in seven sentences, certainly in seven verses. Here is Luke's account of it:

> The God of the people of Israel chose our ancestors; he made the people prosper during their stay in Egypt; with mighty power he led them out of that country; for about forty years he endured their conduct in the wilderness; and he overthrew seven nations in Canaan, giving their land to his people as their inheritance. All this took about 450 years.
>
> After this, God gave them judges until the time of Samuel the prophet. Then the people asked for a king, and he gave them Saul son of Kish, of the tribe of Benjamin,

who ruled forty years. After removing Saul, he made David their king. God testified concerning him: *"I have found David son of Jesse, a man after my own heart; he will do everything I want him to do."*

From this man's descendants God has brought to Israel the Savior Jesus, as he promised. (Acts 13:17-23; my italics)

Can you see the sequence?

> Abraham ("our ancestors") → exodus → wilderness → land → judges → monarchy → David

When he gets to David, Paul quotes that verse that we have chosen for our fourth sentence about how David is "a man after my own heart." Then Paul jumps straight from David to Jesus. We won't be doing that in this book (we'd be short on the sentences, and there's a lot more Old Testament after David—which Paul knew perfectly well, of course). But the fact that Paul makes this direct link from David to Christ is very important. A little later in his sermon, Paul claims that Jesus of Nazareth is the promised son of David, the Messiah. But unlike David (who dies and is buried. Period), Jesus dies and is buried *and is raised to life in glorious resurrection*. Because of his resurrection, Jesus is the one to whom the words first spoken to David truly apply: "You are my Son, today I have become your Father" (Psalm 2:7). Jesus is the one who will be the true King, not only over Israel but over all nations on earth as the very next verse of Psalm 2 declares: "Ask me, and I will make the nations your inheritance, the ends of the earth your possession" (Psalm 2:8). Messiah Jesus, risen son of David, is Lord and King of all creation. As Paul summarizes in Romans 1:2-4 (and see also 2 Timothy 2:8), this is at the heart of Paul's gospel.

There is another reason for choosing David for our fourth sentence (not just because it's good to follow the example of the apostle Paul). Remember the sequence of covenants that we have observed so far: first Noah, then Abraham, then Moses (Sinai)? Now we come to the next most-important covenant in the Bible—God's covenant with David, sometimes called the Davidic covenant. It is described in 2 Samuel 7, and it constitutes God's promise that a son of David will always reign over the people of Israel. That points us forward, through the long line of kings that follow David (we'll have a quick look at them in the next chapter), ultimately of course to Jesus, David's greater Son. But it also makes a strong contrast with what goes on before David turns up—the depressing centuries of Israel's early life in the land of Canaan, the repeated unfaithfulness of the people, the chaos and anarchy of the era of the judges, and especially the tragic failure of the first king, Saul. Against that dark background, our fourth sentence shines out. God finds in David a man after his own heart.

We need to be clear what that expression means in its original language and context. In English the expression "a man after my own heart" has come to mean "somebody I really like; somebody I get on well with; my favorite person." But in Hebrew the heart is not so much the center of emotions and feelings. It is the seat of the will and decisions. God is not saying that David will be his special favorite (God has to discipline David very severely later on). Rather, it means that David will be the ruler who will carry out God's plans and purpose at that time in Israel's history—instead of all the failing ones before him (apart from Samuel). That is exactly how Paul interprets his quotation from 1 Samuel 13:14, by adding a phrase from Isaiah 44:28: "He will do everything I want him to do." In that sense our fourth sentence, originally written about David, applies even more completely to Jesus—the one God appointed as ruler and who did indeed accomplish all God sent him to do. That connection was probably in the back of Paul's mind also.

However, even Paul does not skip from Moses to David without briefly filling in what came in between, so neither should we. Maybe history isn't your thing, and you may like to head straight to the section "The Davidic Covenant" that follows. However, I'd encourage you to come back before too long and read the next few sections for two reasons. First, Paul insists (him again) that "all Scripture is God-breathed and is useful" (2 Timothy 3:16), and that applies to the history books too. Second, as we said in the introduction, *this story is our story*. We belong to this people, and "these things happened to them as examples and were written down as warnings for us" (1 Corinthians 10:11).

Let's travel with Israel from Sinai to Solomon. We ended the last chapter with God making his covenant with Israel and giving them his law at Mount Sinai (Exodus 19–24). But immediately after that, from Exodus 25 onwards, most of the book is taken up with God's instructions for the building of the tabernacle, as it is called in most English Bibles (Exodus 25–31), and then (after the terrible incident of the golden calf, in Exodus 32–34) the account of it being built and God's glory coming to fill it (Exodus 35–40).

The Tabernacle

The tabernacle was designed to be a kind of portable sanctuary. It was an ornate tent stretched over a wooden framework, with an inner lining of very beautiful woven fabric and outer skins that made it weatherproof. The descriptions in Exodus look complicated, but in fact the structure and its contents are relatively simple. They needed to be, since the whole arrangement had to be easy to put together, take apart, and carry with them on their travels. It had three main sections.

THE TABERNACLE

HOLY OF HOLIES

Ark of the
Covenant

Veil

Altar of Incense

Menorah

Table of
Shewbread

HOLY PLACE

Tent Entrance

Laver

Altar of
Burnt Offerings

OUTER COURTYARD

Entrance

There was an outer rectangular courtyard enclosed with fabric suspended from poles. This was the place where people met for animal sacrifices conducted by the priests. There was an altar for that purpose and a large bath for ritual washing.

There was the outer part of the main tent itself, known as the Holy Place. It housed a smaller altar for burning incense, a table with loaves of bread placed on it, and a seven-branched oil-lamp.

There was the inner room, the Most Holy Place, at the far end of the tent, perfectly cubic in shape. It contained the Ark of the Covenant with the two tablets of the Ten Commandments inside, and a cover known as the atonement cover. This place symbolized the most holy presence of God himself (though there was no image of God there, of course). Only the high priest could enter that part of the tent, and only once a year on the Day of Atonement (Leviticus 16).

What is the purpose of it all? There is an immediate meaning for Israel as well as a broader significance in the Bible as a whole.

God's dwelling place. For Israel, the tent is the focal point of the presence of God—visibly and almost tangibly dwelling in the midst of his people. It is the place where Moses (especially and intimately) and the rest of the people can meet with God in worship and sacrifice; in fact, it is referred to several times as the tent of meeting. Here is how God himself describes the purpose of this place:

> There I will meet you and speak to you; there also I will meet with the Israelites, and the place will be consecrated by my glory.
>
> So I will consecrate the tent of meeting and the altar and will consecrate Aaron and his sons to serve me as priests. *Then I will dwell among the Israelites and be their God. They will know that I am the LORD their God, who brought*

them out of Egypt so that I might dwell among them. I am the LORD their God. (Exodus 29:42-46; my italics)

Can you see the emphasis on both redemption ("out of Egypt") and covenant ("I am the LORD their God"), and the purpose of it all—so that God can dwell in the midst of this people? Moses realizes that this (having God dwelling in the midst of his people) is what makes Israel distinct from other nations, as an essential part of its missional identity and role in God's plans (Exodus 33:15-16).

In a wider biblical perspective, the tent (and the temple that later replaced it in the reign of Solomon) is a kind of microcosm—that is, a mini-universe in which heaven and earth could meet. Creation itself as a whole ("heaven and earth") was intended to be the place of God's dwelling with us. But our sin and rebellion resulted in a fracture between heaven and earth. This does not, of course, mean that God is not involved with what happens on earth. Rather, his "resting place" is now heaven, while the earth is his "footstool" (Isaiah 66:1-2). The tent and then the temple provide a singular place where heaven and earth can once again come together.

Later in the Bible, the New Testament presents Jesus himself as Immanuel—God dwelling with us. Messiah Jesus embodies the temple (John 2:19-22), and the church also functions as the place of God's dwelling (Ephesians 2:19-22; 1 Peter 2:4-5). Until finally, in the new creation, there will be no need of a physical temple, for the whole creation will once again be filled with the glory and presence of God among his redeemed people (Revelation 21:1-3, 22-23).

Priests and sacrifice. Priests are appointed to serve in the tabernacle area and perform other duties in the community. They are initially Aaron (Moses' brother) and his sons, and then his descendants within the tribe of Levi. They have a wide range of responsibilities, including teaching God's law to the people (Leviticus 10:10-11) and diagnosing issues of public health (Leviticus 13–15). But their main job is to offer the sacrifices of the people at the altar in the courtyard of the tabernacle and later the temple.

The system of sacrifices is described in Leviticus 1–7. There are different regulations for five different kinds of sacrifice, serving different but complementary purposes. The overall intention is to cleanse the community from the effects of routine (or unintentional) sins and ritual uncleanness for various reasons. The names given here are from the NIV, but different Bibles have variations.

The burnt offering. The sacrificial animal is wholly consumed on the altar. This sacrifice is offered both in relation to atonement for wrongdoing and in thanksgiving and worship generally.

The grain offering. This seems to accompany other sacrifices.

The fellowship offering. The meat of the sacrificed animal is shared, both as a happy feast for the worshipers and as a source of food for the priests. This expresses renewed fellowship between the worshiper and their family and God.

The sin offering. This also has atoning significance and is also used for ritual cleansing.

The guilt offering. This accompanies reparation for wrongs done to others.

Burnt offerings and fellowship offerings are the commonest kinds of sacrifice. The sacrificial system impresses on the people that although Yahweh is their God and wants to dwell in the midst of his people and maintain a loving and protective relationship with them, Yahweh is utterly holy and cannot be approached lightly by sinful people. Sin and uncleanness have to be dealt with and atoned for before people can come into God's presence in worship and thanksgiving.

The Wilderness

After staying at Mount Sinai approximately two years, Israel sets off toward the land God has promised them (Numbers 10:11-13). From the oasis at Kadesh Barnea, Moses sends out twelve spies to reconnoiter the land, but they return with a ten-to-two verdict against trying to invade it. The people's morale fails; they refuse to trust in God's promise to go with them and defeat their enemies, and they rebel against Moses and will not go up into the land. The story is recorded in Numbers 13–14, but it is worth also reading Moses' recollection and interpretation of the tragic event in Deuteronomy 1:19-46.

The result is that all the people who have come out of Egypt stay in the wilderness for the next thirty-eight years until almost all of them die, and it is the next generation that eventually crosses the Jordan into the land. That era in the wilderness is filled with both negative and positive memories for Israel.

On the one hand, it is a time of constant grumbling and rebellion against God, as recorded in the book of Numbers. The Israelites are the people God has chosen to be the means of bringing blessing to all nations, but they themselves are as sinful as any others. They repeatedly incur God's judgment and are in constant need of God's mercy. In that sense, they represent fallen humanity at its worst. We read their stories with some horror, but not with any sense of moral superiority. On the contrary, we should be surprised at how honestly Israel portrays the epic history of their own ancestors in such dark colors.

On the other hand, the wilderness is a time when Israel experiences the astounding grace of God. He leads them and feeds them and waters them. He protects them from their enemies and from those who want to curse them. He spares them even when they make him angry enough to destroy them. You can read some of that story in Exodus 16–17 and Numbers 11; 22–25, but it is easier to read the summaries in Deuteronomy 1–3; 8. This is something that Israel is told to remember forever, as a profound learning experience that should influence the way they will live in the land:

> Remember how the LORD your God led you all the way in the wilderness these forty years, to humble and test you in order to know what was in your heart, whether or not you would keep his commands. He humbled you, causing you to hunger and then feeding you with manna, which neither you nor your ancestors had known, to teach you that man does not live on bread alone but on every word that comes from the mouth of the LORD. Your clothes did not wear out and your feet did not swell during these forty years. Know then in your heart that as a man disciplines his son, so the LORD your God disciplines you. (Deuteronomy 8:2-5; I also recommend reading the rest of the chapter)

Sadly, they forget much more than they remember, and later prophets will recall the wilderness years as almost a honeymoon period in comparison to the later unfaithfulness of the people (Jeremiah 2:1-8; Hosea 11:1-4). Those verses in Deuteronomy, however, clearly made a deep impression on the Lord Jesus Christ during his forty days in the wilderness, during which he determines, as the Son of God, to obey where Israel disobeyed and to be faithful to his Father's will where they had been unfaithful and rebellious (Matthew 4:1-4).

The Land of Canaan

The book of Joshua opens with words that we might have wondered whether we were ever going to hear. At last, God tells the people, under their new leader, Joshua, to get up and cross the River Jordan and take possession of the land of Canaan. Joshua was Moses' assistant and chief military officer throughout the wilderness period, and after the death of Moses he steps into the leadership for the next phase. God gives him words of instruction and encouragement that have strengthened many new leaders ever since (Joshua 1). Like Moses, Joshua (whose name, like the name Jesus, means "the LORD is salvation"), serves God through his old age until the close of his own generation. Even then, he challenges them to go on choosing and serving Yahweh as God in a covenant renewal ceremony at the end of his life (Joshua 23–24).

They cross the River Jordan, and the story is told in a way that echoes the crossing of the sea when the previous generation left Egypt (Joshua 3–4). Then Joshua leads rapid military campaigns in the center, the south, and the north of the country, attacking and destroying the small city-forts of the local kings. This breaks the political and military control of those nations over the land, but there follows a long period of slow possession and settlement that goes on for many years. Some of the territory, including the city of Jerusalem, is not captured until the time of King David. Nevertheless, the boundaries of the tribal settlements are mapped out in the second half of the book of Joshua, even though some of them remain rather idealistic, as the book of Judges will show.

The book of Joshua is clearly not a typical portrayal of some epic conquest in which one side is glorified and the other demonized. The hero is not Israel, nor even Joshua, but God himself. The question is not "Whose side is God on?" but rather "Who is on the LORD's side?" (see Joshua 5:13-14). We need to always keep in mind that Israel exists to serve the purpose of God (not the other way around). When they step outside that purpose, they feel his wrath. Conversely, when others align themselves with God's purpose, they meet his mercy.

GENOCIDE?

Many people are deeply troubled by the Old Testament's accounts of the conquest of Canaan by the Israelites. Did God really command such violence? How can it be reconciled with what we know about God's compassion and love? These are real problems and cannot be adequately handled here. But here at least are some brief perspectives that need to be kept in mind. They do not solve all the problems but help us see beyond our immediate reactions.[1]

The conquest was a limited military event, confined to a single generation. Most of the other wars in the Old Testament were not commanded by God, and some were condemned.

There was a rhetoric of warfare in the ancient world that used graphic hyperbole ("killing everything that breathed") when the reality on the ground was known to be much less. (We use the same kind of hyperbole in sport, when we boast about our team "annihilating" the opposition—we know the word is exaggerated and not literal.)

The book of Judges shows that the picture of total destruction in Joshua was in fact only partial. The biblical editors did not see a contradiction between the rhetoric and the reality.

What was attacked and destroyed were the small city-forts, with their kings and soldiers—the military power of the Canaanites. Most of the ordinary population seem either to have moved out to the hills or in some cases moved over to join the Israelites.

The Bible explains that God used the Israelites as agents of his judgment on the wickedness of the Canaanites by that time (Leviticus 18:24-30; Deuteronomy 9:1-6). This was *not* just random genocide and land grab, but the exercise of God's moral justice.

Later, God exercises the same justice *against* Israel by using their enemies as agents of judgment on them—in fact, he does so far more often against Israel than against Canaan.

The defeat of the Canaanite enemies is celebrated throughout the rest of the Old Testament as a righteous act of God, as part of the history of salvation. We cannot surgically cut it out as primitive violence.

Neither Jesus nor any New Testament writer raises any question or embarrassment over this part of their Scriptures.

That principle is illustrated in two of the early stories in the book, which are intentionally surprising. We have been led to expect that Israel will drive out or exterminate all the Canaanites. Yet the first Canaanite we meet in the book is a converted one who gets saved—Rahab. Her profession of faith in the God of Israel gives her protection (Joshua 2:8-14; 6:22-25; see also Hebrews 11:31; James 2:25-26). Is she exceptional, or are there others who similarly come over to the Lord's side?

In the story of Achan we meet an Israelite who disobeys God and is effectively treated like a Canaanite, expelled and executed (Joshua 7). Israel is learning that God's door is open to foreigners who turn to him, and learning at the same time that merely being an Israelite by birth and tribal identity is no guarantee of salvation if one falls into lies, deceit, and disobedience.

TRIBES AND JUDGES

For approximately two centuries after Joshua, the tribes of Israel struggle to keep hold of the land they have entered. This is known as the period of the judges, since the leaders of the people are known by that term. However, the term (in Hebrew) does not mean somebody sitting in a courtroom but a leader in general terms—sometimes exercising military leadership in battle, sometimes putting things right in the community by making judicial decisions, sometimes giving spiritual guidance to the people. The book of Judges shows us several things about this rather chaotic era that help us appreciate the enormous change that takes place when God finds, in David, a man after his own heart.

Disunity. For a long time the tribes of Israel are absorbed with their own struggles to hold on to and expand the land they have captured from the Canaanites in the initial invasion. They are isolated from one another by the mountainous nature of the country and by the parts still controlled by the Canaanites. They

THE LAND

The land becomes one of the major themes in the faith of Old Testament Israel, an essential part of God's promise to Abraham, as we saw in chapter two. Israel believed two complementary things about their land.

It was the land God gave. Israel had a land to live in, quite simply, because God promised it and then gave it to them. This land-gift tradition taught Israel something very important: God was dependable. He had kept his promise to Abraham. God's faithfulness to his promise had overcome all the obstacles: oppression and slavery in Egypt, the grumblings and rebellions of the Israelites, the attacks of their enemies, and the resistance of the Canaanites. The land was tangible proof of the character of God. Every harvest reminded the Israelites that God could be trusted, and they were totally dependent on that fact. As an Israelite farmer brought the firstfruits of his harvest to the sanctuary, he affirmed this truth with gratitude and rejoicing (Deuteronomy 26:1-11).

It was the land God still owned. Israel had possession of the land, but God remained the ultimate owner—as he does for all the earth (Psalm 24:1). It was as if Yahweh were the great landlord and Israel his tenants. That is how God himself describes the relationship: "The land is mine," says the Lord, "and you are my guests and tenants" (Leviticus 25:23; my translation). What this meant in practice was that God cared about everything to do with life on his land, as the many economic laws in the Torah show: how it was to be shared out among the tribes and families, and not just bought and sold in a commercial way; what was to be done with its produce, especially for the poor and needy; how those who worked on the land (human and animal) were to be treated; and how they were to deal with issues of poverty and debt. This explains why the prophets, speaking in God's name, were so angry at the suffering caused by economic injustice and oppression, as some people accumulated vast estates while others were driven off their land altogether. It also explains why the climax of God's judgment on Israel was to drive them out of the land again into exile in Babylon, and why the proof of his forgiveness and restoration was when he enabled them to return to the land about fifty years later. The land was a pivotal part of Israel's identity and covenant responsibility.

have no capital city, no king, no national army. They come under frequent attack from surrounding nations. Sometimes they fight disastrously with one another.

Yet they manage through this era to hold on to some sense of unity. They have a common ideal identity as *Israel*, such that they belong to one another and feel some moral obligation to come to one another's help. This is illustrated in the stories of Deborah (see Judges 4–5, especially Judges 5:6-18) and Gideon (Judges 6:33-35). They have a common identity as the people of *Yahweh*. He is their real king and supreme judge, even above local leaders. This religious allegiance is centered on Shiloh where the tabernacle and the Ark of the Covenant are stationed. The Israelite tribes are in the land but not yet a unified nation, nor in control of all the territory.

Disloyalty. The book of Judges is a depressing read, for it records how the Israelites repeatedly turn away from Yahweh their God to worship the gods of the surrounding Canaanites. The sequence is summarized in Judges 2:6-23. You may wonder how they can be so frequently disloyal, but try to understand how they are tempted to think.

Baal is the name of the dominant god of Canaan, the land the Israelites have come to live in. The inhabitants of the land seem to find him pretty powerful—just look at their success in agriculture, commerce, civilization (why, they have even invented an alphabet), cities, things the Israelites, after generations of slavery in Egypt and a generation in the wilderness, have little expertise in. The Israelites probably feel that they can do with the help of whatever gods are around. Baal is claimed to be the god of rain, fertility (of the land and your crops), of sex and procreation, of business, and of the land itself. To be frank, Baal is the god of everything that seems to matter. As for Yahweh—he is a pretty competent god to have in battle, as their history shows, and they will not abandon him altogether (they think). But for everyday, practical life in the real world of living in this land, you really need Baal. Or so it seems.

That is the essence of *syncretism*, mixing the worship of the living God with the gods of the people around. Before we blame the ancient Israelites, are modern Christians much different? On Sunday—sure, we worship the God we know through the Bible and Jesus Christ. But for the rest of the week, our lives are easily governed by the idols of our surrounding culture—success, money, status, technology, consumerism, celebrity, and so on. The Israelites find such a mixture is fundamentally disloyalty to their covenant God and redeemer.

Deliverance. What stands out in the book of Judges, however, is not so much the repeated failure of the Israelites as the great acts of God in delivering them. He does this through a sequence of remarkable men and women. Who are they, and why are they called judges?

They are raised up by God. They are not self-appointed (one tries and comes to a very sticky end in Judges 9), nor are they democratically elected. It is God who takes the initiative and calls them into their roles.

They are God's special agents. They act on God's behalf, with God's authority, so that really it is God acting through them as the real leader of his people.

They carry out God's justice. Sometimes that includes judicial activity as we know it, but the scope of God's justice is wider than merely legal affairs. If his people are being oppressed, then there is injustice. In raising up leaders to defeat such oppressors, God is acting in justice, and his agents are called judges, doing God's justice on earth.

They act in the power of God's Spirit. Some of them are very ordinary people, not great superheroes by any means. When they achieve great things, it is because the Spirit of God is at work. Gideon is a good example: he protests that he is the least in his family, but we read that "the Spirit of God clothed Gideon" (Judges 6:34; my literal translation) and so he is able to defeat the Midianites.

They become examples of faith. The letter to the Hebrews includes some of the Old Testament judges in its list of examples of faith (Hebrews 11:32). This does not mean they are perfect examples of model behavior. Some of them are very unsavory characters who do strange things. But they respond to God's call in trust and obedience, even against the odds. That is what faith means.

"WE THREE KINGS . . ."

We're getting closer to King David and our fourth sentence, but Israel does not become a monarchy overnight. The transition from the time of the judges is slow. The towering figure who spans that transition is Samuel. The story fills 1 Samuel 1–12.

Samuel. Samuel exercises a lifetime of leadership among the tribes of Israel that is something like a king (though he is not, of course). Saul, the first king, is in many ways similar to the judges who led the people before him. Nevertheless, the definitive change happens at that time: Samuel is the last of the judges, and Saul the first of the kings, and after him comes David, the man after God's own heart. What leads up to this change? Three factors stand out in the narrative.

Samuel's leadership qualities. From his youth, Samuel is an outstanding man of God. He functions as a judge in the legal sense; he is also a robust military leader; he can speak the word of God as a prophet; and he can perform sacrifices like a priest, though not at the tent in Shiloh (where Eli and his sons are priests). Sadly, however, his own sons do not live up to his high standards or follow his example, but give in to the temptations of bribery and corruption. Ironically, Samuel's excellent model of leadership contributes to the demand for a king.

The Philistines. These are the worst of any of the enemies that the Israelites have had to face. They are also an invading people from the Aegean region who have settled on the western coastal plain. They are already using iron technology and so have superior weapons and chariots. The Philistines treat the Hebrew tribesmen with contempt. They not only beat them in battle, but even temporarily steal the Ark of the Covenant as well. The Israelites, deeply humiliated, feel that their only hope lies in having a strong unified leadership—a king.

The people's demand. Representatives of the tribes come to Samuel and ask him to appoint a king for them. We can understand the pressures behind the request, but it does not please Samuel—or God—for two reasons. First, the people say they want a king in order to be "like the other nations." But God has called Israel precisely to be different from other nations, not just religiously but also in their social, economic, and political arrangements. Second, the people's desire for a human king is an implied rejection of the kingship of God, exercised through the leaders he has raised up in times of need. God says to Samuel, "It's not you; it's me. I am the one they have rejected as their king."

God gives them a king as they asked. But not before Samuel makes very clear to them some of the long-term negative consequences they will face under a monarchical system of government. They will suffer things they have not under the old tribal system, including taxation, forced labor, confiscation of land, conscription—until in the end monarchy will feel like slavery all over again (1 Samuel 8:10-18). As it turns out later, Samuel's warnings come grimly true, as early as the reign of the third king, Solomon, and get even worse after him.

To sum it all up: The change to monarchy in Israel is an ambiguous and paradoxical thing. Israel's request for a king is in itself the result of sinful lack of faith and willingness to embrace its identity as God's holy (different) people. As the rest of the Old Testament shows, almost every king fails, morally and spiritually, and sometimes politically too—disastrously in the end. Nevertheless, God accepts the request and responds to it. He chooses their first king, and then the next one—David himself. Furthermore, he promises to bless the king and the nation if both continue to obey him as the covenant requires. But if they do not, then both will suffer God's judgment. In the longer perspective, God will use the model of human kingship (flawed though it is) as a vehicle for some very important teaching about his own status as the divine King, and also as a way of preparing for the one who will come as the truly anointed Messiah King of God's people.

Kingship in Israel, then, illustrates very powerfully an important part of the theology of the Old Testament (and the Bible): the interaction of human choices and God's sovereignty. On the one hand, kingship emerges as something fallen, flawed, and even a rejection of God's rule. Yet, on the other hand, God in his own sovereign providence accepts it, works with and through it, and builds it into his long-term saving plan, turning it into a model for understanding one part of the identity of Jesus Christ.

King Saul. Saul is one of the most tragic figures in the Bible. His story occupies the rest of 1 Samuel.

Israel's first king is as ambiguous as the office he takes on. On the one hand, he has many gifts, is tall and strong, has the initial friendship and support of Samuel, and wins some successful battles. But, on the other hand, he has some fatal flaws as well. He fails to follow carefully what Samuel tells him, makes some very foolish decisions (and even admits his own folly), falls into a paranoid and murderous jealousy of David, ends up in such spiritual loneliness that he tries to get help from the dead Samuel through a female medium (a practice he himself has banned), and finally takes his own life as his troops are routed by the Philistines (again). The Israelites asked for a king to drive out the Philistines. But when their first king dies, they are more under the cruel oppression of the Philistines than ever.

King David. After Saul dies, there is a long and nasty civil war, but eventually David (who was anointed by Samuel years before) is acknowledged as king. He rules for seven years at Hebron in the land of his own tribe, Judah. But then he takes a step that will have great significance for the rest of human history: he captures the small mountain city of Jerusalem from its Jebusite inhabitants and makes it the fortified capital of his kingdom. Strategically, it is a superb choice; it is fairly central in the land and easily defended. David builds himself a palace there and makes it the center of his kingdom—that is, of all the tribes of Israel (2 Samuel 2–5). He reigns there in Jerusalem for another thirty-three years.

Secure in this capital, David organizes a system of government and defeats many of the surrounding nations, making them pay tribute to him (so he accumulates a lot of wealth). Above all, he decisively defeats the Philistines and gives the people rest from their enemies. At last—several centuries after Moses and Joshua—the Israelites are in control of the Promised Land.

He also brings the Ark of the Covenant to Jerusalem, amid great popular rejoicing (2 Samuel 6). He wants to build a temple to house it, but God tells him that that task will be for his son to accomplish. Very soon, Jerusalem becomes known not only as the city of David but as Zion, the city of God. It becomes the focal point for the faith and worship of the tribes of Israel.

David, the man after God's own heart, has indeed accomplished great things.

But once again, the Bible's honesty is clear. David falls into a web of sin that includes adultery, deception, and planned murder—the story of David and Bathsheba in 2 Samuel 11–12. Though David repents, the consequences of his failure poison his own family life thereafter. He has no moral authority to rebuke one of his sons for the same kind of behavior. Another of his sons, Absalom, wages war against his father, a war that costs him his own life, to David's terrible sorrow (2 Samuel 13–18).

The books of Chronicles record how, before his death, David provides his son, Solomon, with plans to build a temple for the God of Israel. It is also a record of immense resources of wealth, David's and the people's (1 Chronicles 28–29).

King Solomon. After a short but bloody period of ruthless elimination of his rivals, Solomon settles down to a reign that is long and glorious, but with a dark underside. The story fills 1 Kings 1–11.

On the positive side, Solomon develops an administrative system for the whole country and fortifies some defensive cities. He gives Israel a period free from wars that it has never known before—or ever will again. He gains an international reputation for his wealth and wisdom, turning Jerusalem into a center of culture and cosmopolitan trade and diplomacy. He engages in building projects and commercial ventures. Above all, he builds the temple that his father, David, planned. He dedicates it with a remarkable prayer (1 Kings 8), asking God to hear the prayers not only of his people Israel but also of any foreigners who come to the temple and pray there to Yahweh the God of Israel. Why should God answer the prayers of *foreigners*? So that the name of Yahweh will become known to the ends of the earth—a missional motivation that echoes the Abrahamic covenant (1 Kings 8:41-43).

On the negative side, Solomon antagonizes the northern tribes, who do not like being ruled by the arrogant tribe of Judah alone in the South. He fulfills the worst of Samuel's predictions, imposing taxes and forced labor, creating divisions between rich and poor in the country that get worse as time goes on, and

generating much discontent and bitterness. Worst of all, in spite
of building the temple to Yahweh, he endangers the simplicity of
Israel's faith by multiple foreign marriages and political alliances—
which include importing the worship of other gods. In short,
Solomon breaks all three of the restrictions that God placed on
kings in Israel. Deuteronomy 17:14-20 says that an Israelite king
should not multiply for himself weapons, women, and wealth (the
very things that were expected perks of political power in other
nations, including today). Solomon multiplies all three.

Shortly after Solomon's death, in 930 BC, the anger of the
northern tribes at the oppressive policies of the Jerusalem court
boils over. They rebel against Solomon's son Rehoboam and split
off to form a separate kingdom in the North—the kingdom of
Israel, in distinction from the kingdom of Judah in the South.
God's people are divided. The wounds go deep.

The united monarchy (that is, kingship over all the tribes)
exercised by Saul, David, and Solomon lasted just about one
century. The man after God's own heart played his part in his
own generation, but his own sins and the increasing sins of the
people produce one series of disasters after another.

The Davidic Covenant

The most important event during this period is the covenant
God makes with David. The account is in 2 Samuel 7. Here is the
key section.

> The LORD declares to you [David] that the LORD himself
> will establish a house for you: When your days are over and
> you rest with your ancestors, I will raise up your offspring
> to succeed you, your own flesh and blood, and I will es-
> tablish his kingdom. He is the one who will build a house
> for my Name, and I will establish the throne of his kingdom

forever. I will be his father, and he will be my son. When he does wrong, I will punish him with a rod wielded by men, with floggings inflicted by human hands. But my love will never be taken away from him, as I took it away from Saul, whom I removed from before you. Your house and your kingdom will endure forever before me; your throne will be established forever. (2 Samuel 7:11-16)

David says he wants to build a house for God. God replies that he doesn't need one (though he will allow David's son to build one anyway—Solomon's temple). Rather, God will build a house for David, meaning a royal dynasty.

God's covenant promise to David, as you can see in the previous passage, includes four things:

1. One of David's descendants will be king over Israel continuously into the future. The first is David's son Solomon.

2. The sons of David, who will be kings over Israel, will be regarded as sons of God, which does not mean they are divine but that God will take them into a relationship with himself like father and son (Psalm 2:7).

3. That father-son relationship includes reciprocal love (of God) and obedience (of the king), with the threat of punishment (just like the covenant with Israel). Thus the Davidic king is still accountable to God for keeping God's law. In that sense, the covenant with David does not *replace* the Sinai covenant, but rather puts the king under the same obligations as the rest of the people. Yahweh is still Israel's true king. And Israel's human king, like the people he rules over, must obey Yahweh.

4. David's house and kingdom will be forever. That means a son of David will rule over God's people forever.

This promise is so astonishing that David himself has to sit down to take it in before thanking God for such generosity in a remarkable prayer (2 Samuel 7:18-29). When this promise to David is combined with the glory of Solomon's temple, it generates a whole outpouring of worship and praise connected to *Zion*—city of David and city of God. Indeed, there is a whole collection of psalms of Zion scattered through Israel's songbook. Here's just a sample of the emotions that Jerusalem-Zion-temple generated in the hearts of devout worshiping Israelites. These psalms and others like them are all the result of David's decision to choose Jerusalem as his capital city and provide for his son to build a temple there for the Lord, and God's decision to make his covenant promise to David and his house.

> Great is the LORD, and most worthy of praise,
>   in the city of our God, his holy mountain.
> Beautiful in its loftiness,
>   the joy of the whole earth,
> like the heights of Zaphon is Mount Zion,
>   the city of the Great King. (Psalm 48:1-2)

> How lovely is your dwelling place,
>   LORD Almighty!
> My soul yearns, even faints,
>   for the courts of the LORD;
> my heart and my flesh cry out
>   for the living God. (Psalm 84:1-2)

> He has founded his city on the holy mountain.
> The LORD loves the gates of Zion
>   more than all the other dwellings of Jacob.
> Glorious things are said of you,
>   city of God. (Psalm 87:1-3)

For the LORD has chosen Zion,
>   he has desired it for his dwelling, saying,
> "This is my resting place for ever and ever;
>   here I will sit enthroned, for I have desired it."
>   (Psalm 132:13-14)

Two big problems arise, however. *First: the problem of complacency.* The people are so aware of God's promise to the line of David, so sure that God has chosen Jerusalem as the place where he will dwell, so confident that God will always defend his city and temple, that they fall into a complacent arrogance. God will never allow his city and temple to be destroyed, they think, no matter how the king and the people live. Centuries after David, therefore, the prophet Jeremiah has to warn David's descendants, who are kings in Jerusalem and are behaving with blatant wickedness, that they are not immune to God's judgment. God will keep his threats as well as his promises (Jeremiah 7:1-5; 22:1-30). As we shall see in the next chapter, he does.

Second: the problem of failure. Almost every one of the kings in the line of David, starting with Solomon and with only two exceptions (Hezekiah and Josiah), fails to live in obedience to God, as son to father. Solomon's son Rehoboam acts with such oppressive folly that he loses four-fifths of his kingdom, leaving the kingdom of Judah as a small remnant of the original twelve tribes. In the end, after centuries of warnings from the prophets, the last king in the line of David, King Zedekiah, loses his kingdom, his city, his sons, and his life in the terrible conflagration when Nebuchadnezzar, king of Babylon, destroys Jerusalem and takes the people into exile in 587 BC.

David's kingdom has fallen. Has God's promise to David failed, the promise made to the man after God's own heart? That is the agonizing question about which you can read very luridly in Psalm 89, written in the aftermath of the catastrophe of 587 BC. The glorious first part celebrates God's promises to David (Psalm 89:1-37). But then we are shocked by the accusing questions in the second part (Psalm 89:38-51), ending with "Lord, where is your former great love, which in your faithfulness you swore to David?" (Psalm 89:49). Where indeed?

But no. God has not forgotten his promise. There is no son of David reigning in Jerusalem any more (in fact, there is no kingdom of Judah or kingdom of Israel any more either). But God has *not* abandoned his promise to David. Rather, that promise is transformed into an expectation, a prophetic declaration, that God will *once again in the future* raise up a son of David who will be the true king and shepherd of God's people, and that *his* kingdom will indeed be eternal. This becomes the great hope of Israel and its Scriptures.

Here are some of the texts in the prophets that express that hope of a coming son of David and his universal and eternal reign:

> For to us a child is born,
>   to us a son is given,
>   and the government will be on his shoulders.
> And he will be called
>   Wonderful Counselor, Mighty God,
>   Everlasting Father, Prince of Peace.
> Of the greatness of his government and peace
>   there will be no end.
> He will reign on David's throne
>   and over his kingdom,
> establishing and upholding it
>   with justice and righteousness
>   from that time on and forever.

The zeal of the LORD Almighty
> will accomplish this. (Isaiah 9:6-7)

A shoot will come up from the stump of Jesse [the father
> of David];
>> from his roots a Branch will bear fruit.
The Spirit of the LORD will rest on him—
>> the Spirit of wisdom and of understanding,
>> the Spirit of counsel and of might,
>> the Spirit of the knowledge and fear of the LORD—
and he will delight in the fear of the LORD.

He will not judge by what he sees with his eyes,
> or decide by what he hears with his ears;
but with righteousness he will judge the needy,
> with justice he will give decisions for the poor of the
>> earth. (Isaiah 11:1-4)

"The days are coming," declares the LORD,
> "when I will raise up for David a righteous Branch,
a King who will reign wisely
> and do what is just and right in the land.
In his days Judah will be saved
> and Israel will live in safety.
This is the name by which he will be called:
> The Lord Our Righteous Savior." (Jeremiah 23:5-6)

Micah predicts that the future king of Israel will be born in Bethlehem, the village from which David came (Micah 5:2-4), and his rule will extend to the ends of the earth.

Those passages will sound familiar if you've attended carol services in churches at Christmas. Christians believe that these prophecies, based on that original promise to David, have indeed been fulfilled in Jesus of Nazareth, "the Messiah the son of David, the son of Abraham," as Matthew introduces him (Matthew 1:1).

To return to where we started in this chapter, the apostle Paul emphasizes this at the beginning and end of Romans (Romans 1:3; 15:12). At the heart of Paul's gospel is the affirmation that Jesus of Nazareth, crucified and risen, is the one through whom God has fulfilled his promise to Abraham and David—he is indeed great David's greater Son. For that reason, King Jesus is the one who, by his resurrection, is now proclaimed as Lord and King over all earthly rulers to the ends of the earth. Jesus himself claims this global authority (Matthew 28:18-20), and Paul proclaims it and is prepared to suffer the wrath of those earthly rulers in the form of the Roman Empire and its demands for worship of Caesar as Lord.

Recognizing Jesus as the Messiah and true King in the line of David rests not only on what Paul says. We have it on the authority of God the Father himself. For when Jesus is baptized by John the Baptist in the Jordan at the beginning of his public ministry, God's voice from heaven identifies him with words that intentionally echo what God says to King David in Psalm 2:7—"You are my Son, whom I love; with you I am well pleased" (Mark 1:11).

Jesus, Son of David, Son of God, is the man after God's own heart.

- five -

PROPHETS

What does the LORD *require of you*
but to do justice, and to love kindness,
and to walk humbly with your God?

MICAH 6:8 NRSV

I s that all?

Is that all God required of the people of Israel (or requires of us)? Just those three things?

You may have noticed that Exodus, Leviticus, and Deuteronomy are rather thick books, containing (so our Jewish friends tell us) more than six hundred specific laws. And all God requires are *justice, kindness* (or mercy, or faithfulness—the translations differ), and *humility* before God?

Who says?

Well, Micah the prophet actually, but he says he got the word from God himself—"He has shown you, O mortal, what is good," says Micah 6:8. The God who gives over six hundred instructions is happy to condense them to these three. They are possibly the three that Jesus has in mind when he talks about "the more important matters of the law—justice, mercy and faithfulness" (Matthew 23:23).

As we saw in the introduction, this is not the first time we get such a radical summarizing of what God wants from his people. Deuteronomy presents Moses doing the same thing—except he only manages to reduce God's requirements to five. "And now, Israel, what does the LORD your God ask of you but to *fear* the LORD your God, to *walk* in obedience to him, to *love* him, to *serve* the LORD your God with all your heart and with all your soul, and to *observe* the LORD's commands and decrees that I am giving you today for your own good?" (Deuteronomy 10:12-13; my italics).

Fear, walk, love, serve, observe . . . that's it.

Jesus then manages the ultimate reduction, condensing the whole Law and Prophets (virtually the whole of the Old Testament) to the two fundamental commandments he calls the first and second greatest of all in Matthew 22:34-40: (1) "Love the LORD your God" (Deuteronomy 6:5), and (2) "Love your neighbor as yourself" (Leviticus 19:18).

The point of these powerful summaries is to remind us that being in a right relationship with God is not just a matter of check-box compliance with all the instructions and regulations. It is a matter of *fundamental commitment to God himself*, expressed through love and humble submission to God (in vertical relationship) and acting with justice and compassion in human affairs (in horizontal relationship). Such is the essence of the covenant relationship between God and Israel in the Old Testament, and it is the job of the prophets (a thankless job most of the time) to remind the people of this truth.

Our fifth sentence comes from the lips of a prophet, namely, Micah, who confronted the kingdom of Judah in the eighth century BC and has a collection of his messages edited together in the book of his name in the Bible. In this chapter, then, we tackle a major part of the Old Testament library—the prophets.

Who were they? What was their job? When did they live? Does our choice of sentence represent a fair summary of their message?[1]

SPEAKING FOR GOD

We should start by distinguishing between the large number of *people* who were prophets in Israel and the small number (fifteen) of *books* named after prophets included in the Bible.

There were many prophets sent by God throughout the period of the Old Testament, and most of them do not have books named after them. Moses is a prophet. So is his sister Miriam (Exodus 15:20; Micah 6:4). In fact Moses is in some ways the model for all the later prophets (Deuteronomy 18:18). Then there are prophets such as Samuel, Nathan, Elijah, Elisha, and many others who are mentioned in the history books but not named. Some of the most notable prophets are women, such as Miriam and Deborah.

Then there are the fifteen books in the Old Testament that are collections of the messages of particular named prophets. There are three large books, Isaiah, Jeremiah, and Ezekiel, and then the so-called Book of the Twelve.[2] Those twelve are sometimes referred to as Minor Prophets, the ones from Hosea to Malachi. That word *minor* only means that their books are short, not that they themselves are minor or unimportant in the work they did for God in their own day. Some of them are very significant indeed. The Book of the Twelve as a collection is about the same length as the book of Jeremiah.

Prophets are *men and women who speak out for God.* Quite simply, prophets are messengers. They are God's mouthpiece. God speaks his word through them, directly into the ears, minds, and hearts of his people at different times. What the prophet says is what God wants to be said. When they speak they begin or end with words such as "This is what the LORD says."

Today we sometimes use the words *prophet* or *prophetic* to refer to people foretelling the future. "I'm not a prophet," we might say, meaning, "Don't ask me to predict what is going to happen." But the biblical prophets do not spend all their time predicting the future.

The job of the prophets is to speak God's word directly to the people around them, their own generation. They tell the people of Israel what God is thinking and saying about the *present* situation, whatever is going on in their own time. Sometimes, of course, they *do* speak about the future (whether as a warning or an encouragement). But when they do that, it is usually in order to make people think and act differently in the present—for example, to repent and change, or to have faith and obey God. Future predictions, in other words, are intended to affect the present (their own day), not just leave people gazing into the distance. Prophets should be thought of as *forth*tellers, not *fore*tellers.

GETTING THE MESSAGE

We need to understand the kind of language the prophets use. Remember, they are preachers, street communicators. Their words are originally spoken to be *heard*, not just written to be *read*.

Persuasive tactics. The prophets know (from God) that the people are in real danger if they do not change their ways. They also face a lot of opposition, sometimes violent. We should not imagine that they are involved in polite discussions or academic debate. They are out to *persuade* people to believe what they are saying and act accordingly. Sometimes they need to *shock* people into paying attention. For that reason, the language of the prophets might sometimes seem exaggerated, clashing, and controversial. They use sarcasm and mockery. They can be disgusting and offensive too. They say whatever it might take to get the people to listen to them. Sadly, as we know, the Israelites mostly choose to ignore the prophets' words and go their own way to their own destruction. But they can never say they were not warned.

Poetic vividness. The prophets often speak and write in the form of Hebrew poetry (we'll think about Hebrew poetry in the final chapter). If you look at the pages of prophetic books, you can tell the poetic sections by the short and indented lines, as distinct from the blocks of text in prose. Prophetic messages sometimes come in short bursts, using very graphic terms, with unusual phrases and images. That's the nature of poetry. It strives to say a lot in very few words. It would have been easier to remember. Poetry also tends to use language in special ways, with figures of speech, comparisons, metaphors, symbolism, and so on. Poetry has a way of speaking that should not usually be taken literalistically. Rather, we need to search for the intention, the emotion, the message behind the form of the words, and recognize that poetry makes those things even more powerful.

If you have time and a Bible at hand, take a look at Jeremiah 2. I've included some of the chapter below. It is full of poetic imagery and rhetorical questions. It swings wildly from one picture to another, portraying Israel's unfaithfulness and rebellion against God. The language is colorful and vivid. Try reading it aloud, with passion, pausing at the searching questions and scathing comparisons. That's poetry.

The word of the LORD came to me: "Go and proclaim in the hearing of Jerusalem:

"This is what the Lord says:

"'I remember the devotion of your youth,
    how as a bride you loved me
and followed me through the wilderness,
    through a land not sown.

Israel was holy to the Lord,
    the firstfruits of his harvest;
all who devoured her were held guilty,
    and disaster overtook them,'"
    declares the Lord. . . .

"Therefore I bring charges against you again,"
    declares the Lord.
    "And I will bring charges against your children's children.
Cross over to the coasts of Cyprus and look,
    send to Kedar and observe closely;
    see if there has ever been anything like this:
Has a nation ever changed its gods?
    (Yet they are not gods at all.)
But my people have exchanged their glorious God
    for worthless idols.
Be appalled at this, you heavens,
    and shudder with great horror,"
        declares the Lord.
"My people have committed two sins:
They have forsaken me,
    the spring of living water,
and have dug their own cisterns,
    broken cisterns that cannot hold water.
Is Israel a servant, a slave by birth?
    Why then has he become plunder?
Lions have roared;
    they have growled at him.
They have laid waste his land;
    his towns are burned and deserted." . . .

"Long ago you broke off your yoke
    and tore off your bonds;

you said, 'I will not serve you!'
Indeed, on every high hill
   and under every spreading tree
   you lay down as a prostitute.
I had planted you like a choice vine
   of sound and reliable stock.
How then did you turn against me
   into a corrupt, wild vine?
Although you wash yourself with soap
   and use an abundance of cleansing powder,
   the stain of your guilt is still before me,"
   declares the Sovereign LORD.
"How can you say, 'I am not defiled;
   I have not run after the Baals'?
See how you behaved in the valley;
   consider what you have done.
You are a swift she-camel
   running here and there,
a wild donkey accustomed to the desert,
   sniffing the wind in her craving—
   in her heat who can restrain her?
Any males that pursue her need not tire themselves;
   at mating time they will find her."
     (Jeremiah 2:1-3, 9-15, 20-24)

Picture language. The prophets love pictures as much as Jesus loves parables. I mean word pictures, of course. The prophets paint all kinds of images in the mind to express what they mean. They draw comparisons from the world around them, from nature, from plants, animals and birds and insects, the sun, moon and stars, from wind and fire, earthquake and volcano, from music and buildings, and all human relationships. These word pictures are metaphors, powerful ways of communicating truth. They grab your imagination and spark all kinds of connections in your mind.

Jeremiah uses at least a dozen different word pictures to make his points in Jeremiah 2. Can you see his picture of a bride (Jeremiah 2:2), firstfruits (Jeremiah 2:3), a spring and a cistern (Jeremiah 2:13), lions (Jeremiah 2:15), a vine (Jeremiah 2:21), soap (Jeremiah 2:22), camels and donkeys (Jeremiah 2:23-24), and so on? Jeremiah just leaps from one picture to another, engaging our imagination and making his message memorable. In each case we must ask, What point is he making by creating this picture or metaphor?

Words in action. People remember something that they see even better than what they hear, especially if the two are combined. Sometimes God instructs his prophets to deliver a message along with some action or sign that will reinforce it. This might be a simple, everyday kind of thing that in the circumstances demonstrates great faith, such as Jeremiah's purchase of a field in Jeremiah 32. Sometimes it is very dramatic, as when Jeremiah takes a huge clay pot and smashes it to pieces outside the city in the presence of the political leaders (Jeremiah 19). Other examples of acted prophecies include the following:

• Isaiah goes around naked in Jerusalem to portray the shame of captivity that lies ahead (Isaiah 20).

• Jeremiah buys and wears a new linen sash, then buries it until it is rotten and useless to show what Israel has become like in God's sight (Jeremiah 13).

• Jeremiah puts an ox-yoke on his shoulders and bursts into an international diplomatic conference in Jerusalem to tell the ambassadors of other nations to submit to the yoke of Nebuchadnezzar, because God has raised him up for the moment (Jeremiah 27).

- Ezekiel lies on his side "besieging" a model of Jerusalem on a large clay brick to show the first exiles in Babylon that the city will soon be captured and destroyed (Ezekiel 4–5).

Who Are the Prophets?

Let's now meet some of the most significant prophets and set them very briefly in their historical context. We have to do this in order to make sense of their messages. Reading a passage in a prophetic book can be very confusing. It can feel like switching on the radio or TV in the midst of some heated argument. You may understand the words being spoken, but you have no idea what the speakers are talking about because you don't know the context and background. Fortunately, some of the books give us that historical context in their editorial openings by referring to the particular king or kings during whose reigns they prophesied. In this chapter we mention prophets who arose during the period of the divided monarchy (as distinct from the united monarchy of the first three kings). That lasted about three-and-a-half centuries, from approximately 931 BC to 587 BC. It's a confusing period, since the Bible lists the kings in both kingdoms, and sometimes they overlap, and sometimes very inconsiderately they even have the same name. If you get a comfortable armchair and a very large coffee sometime you can read the whole story from 1 Kings 12 through 2 Kings 25. Then you can read it again, with some different emphases from an account written later, in 2 Chronicles 10–36. Now there's a challenge.

Ninth-century prophets. Two prophets, Elijah and Elisha, arise in the Northern Kingdom of Israel in the ninth century Before Christ. The Northern Kingdom has split from Judah during the reign of Rehoboam, son of Solomon, as a result of the pent-up bitterness and discontent among the northern tribes of Israel against the increasingly heavy cost of Solomon's oppressive

policies. Being more exposed to the pagan nations to the north
(Phoenicia and Syria), the Northern Kingdom of Israel more
rapidly falls into idolatry and especially the cults of the Canaanite god Baal.

Elijah. Elijah's name sums up his life's work. It means "Yahweh
is my God." His mission is to bring Israel back to the worship of
Yahweh alone as the true and living God—not Baal, the Canaanite god whom Queen Jezebel, the Phoenician wife of King
Ahab, is promoting. Elijah's first act is to confront King Ahab
with God's judgment. Because of the nation's sins, the land will
suffer drought for three years. At the end of that time, Elijah arranges a great contest on Mount Carmel between Yahweh and
himself alone on the one side, and all the prophets of Baal on the
other. First Kings 18–19 tells us who wins and what happens
next. Elijah also sees the evil social and economic consequences
of Baal worship. He denounces Ahab and Jezebel for their greedy
and murderous treatment of Naboth and declares that they will
both die under God's judgment.

Elisha. Elisha's name is also significant. It means "God saves."
He is trained as Elijah's assistant and then takes over from him
as God's prophet, leading a small band of prophets in a ministry
that stretches over almost half a century through the reigns of
several kings in the North. God works many miracles through
Elisha. He heals the sick, feeds the hungry, raises the dead, and
delivers a whole city from siege. Jesus says that John the Baptist
is like Elijah, because he calls people to repentance. Just as Elisha
follows Elijah, so Jesus follows John. Jesus' name means the
same: "Yahweh saves." Some of Jesus' miracles remind the people
of the prophet Elisha.

Eighth-century prophets. This is the era of Israel's story when
some truly great prophets arise to bring God's message. We can
select two from the North (Amos and Hosea) and two from the

South (Isaiah and Micah). They are sent by God to the two kingdoms during times of relative prosperity and security: the reign of Jeroboam II in the North, and the kings who follow Uzziah in the South (Jotham, Ahaz, and Hezekiah). In the midst of that prosperity, these prophets see a very different picture underneath: Society is rotten. People are suffering. God is angry.

Amos. Amos is actually from Judah in the South, but God takes him and sends him to preach in the North. He begins by condemning all the surrounding foreign nations—a good way to get people's attention and applause—but then tightens the noose on Israel itself, which would have been shocking. Amos fiercely denounces the social injustices that he sees in the midst of the wealth of some. He defends the exploited poor and calls them "the righteous" (meaning those with right on their side), and he attacks the wealthy, luxury-loving class, especially in Samaria, as "the wicked." This was a very surprising reversal of popular religious understanding of the day. People thought then (as they still do in some places) that to be very rich means you are very blessed by God, no matter how you got your riches. At the same time, Amos claims that the religious rituals that are so popular at the shrines of Bethel and Gilgal are not only *not* pleasing in the sight of God, as the people believe, but actually stink in God's nostrils. The rampant corruption of justice and commercial cheating that is going on in the public square is a complete betrayal of all that God has done for Israel in its history, and also turns their pretended worship into a mockery and an abomination.

Amos is the first in a long line of prophets to have his words remembered and written down in a book bearing his name. Why did that happen? Possibly because his words are so shocking and unexpected, but probably also *because they come true.* His threat that Israel will be destroyed and the people exiled must have sounded ludicrous at the time (when Israel was prosperous and stable). But approximately twenty-five years later, it happens exactly as God warned them through Amos.

The Assyrians, the most powerful empire in the region at the time, besieged and destroyed Samaria in 721 BC. The Israelites of the ten northern tribes were then taken into exile and scattered around the territories of the Assyrian Empire. Foreign peoples from other regions were then brought in to populate the land. The intermingling and intermarriage that happened produced a very mixed kind of community in that central part of Palestine. They eventually became known as the Samaritans and were despised by the people of Judah for centuries, including in Jesus' time.

Hosea. Hosea lived about the same time as Amos, perhaps a little later, and his ministry was mostly directed to the Northern Kingdom. God's message to him comes by way of bitter experience. God tells to him to marry a prostitute named Gomer. She is then unfaithful to him and bears children that are not his own. Hosea sees in his own broken marriage a picture of the pain that Israel's unfaithfulness is causing God. He pictures the covenant relationship between Yahweh and Israel as a marriage—a broken one. Yet God then tells Hosea to buy his former wife back from prostitution and to love her again (imagine paying to get your unfaithful wife back from a pimp). In this costly act of forgiving love, God symbolizes his own gracious faithfulness to his people. There will have to be judgment, but beyond that lies the hope of restoration and a new relationship of love and gratitude.

Hosea shows us something of God's character that many people wrongly think is missing in the Old Testament—his loving tenderness, his desire to forgive, and his longing for an intimate relationship with his people.

Isaiah. Isaiah is like a prince among the prophets. The book in his name is one of the massive mountain peaks of the Bible.

He may have come from a noble family, since he seems to have easy access to the royal court in Jerusalem during the reigns of several kings of Judah in the second half of the eighth century. His role varies from respected adviser to fierce critic.

Isaiah has a lofty vision in the temple of the holiness and majesty of God. Because of this he is bitterly opposed to all forms of human arrogance, whether among the ruling class of his own country or in the military boasting and taunts of the Assyrian Empire.

Isaiah's main message is that Judah should trust Yahweh their God in the midst of the international pressures and dangers of the time and not run off to make useless alliances with other countries such as Egypt or Assyria. King Ahaz rejects such advice. King Hezekiah accepts it. In the longer term, Isaiah foresees that the nation will suffer God's judgment in military defeat and exile. But he also sees beyond that to an era of God's blessing and salvation when Israel will be restored. There will be a new son of David who will reign with justice and bring peace among nations and in nature. Some of these great prophecies are taken up in the New Testament and seen as fulfilled in the birth, life, death, and resurrection of Jesus the Messiah. Others will be fulfilled only when he returns to establish his kingdom and rule over all nations and the whole earth.

Micah. Micah was another prophet in Judah about the same time as Isaiah, and they may well have known each other. They share the same passion for justice, the same strong condemnation of those who are greedily exploiting the poor, and the same vision of God's future reign among all nations. It was Micah who gives us the familiar sentence for this chapter of our book.

Seventh-century prophets. The Assyrian Empire had dominated the whole region of what we now call the Middle East for 150 years. But toward the end of seventh century BC, the Assyrian

Empire collapsed and was replaced by Babylon as the great world power of the region. This ushered in decades of great turbulence in the small kingdom of Judah. King Josiah, in his zeal to bring the people back to loyalty to Yahweh, had brought in some radical purging reforms, creating a lot of distress and opposition in the country. As Assyria's power waned, there was an upsurge of nationalistic fervor in the whole region. Many small nations such as Judah vied for independence after being dominated for so long by Assyria. But at the same time, there was great fear as a new international order was being shaped by the competition between Egypt and Babylon for regional supremacy. Nobody quite knew how things would turn out in the international arena as the old order of the Assyrian Empire fell apart.

Jeremiah. Into that whirlpool of religious, social, and political confusion, God sends a young man named Jeremiah. He grew up in a family of priests in Anathoth, just a few miles from Jerusalem. He knows (from his priestly family background and the Scriptures of the Torah) what kind of faith and life should characterize God's covenant people. But what he sees (from frequent visits to Jerusalem) is that the life of the people from top to bottom of society is a complete denial and travesty of that covenant faith. Showing great courage and suffering constant unpopularity, Jeremiah exposes the lurid sins of his culture with vivid preaching and illustrations. He warns the people that disaster lies ahead (weeping at the thought of it) and urges them repeatedly to repent and change their ways, so as to avoid it. But they refuse.

After the death of King Josiah (whom Jeremiah admires and praises), Jeremiah is hated by the kings who follow—especially King Jehoiakim (who burns a whole scroll full of twenty-three years' worth of Jeremiah's preaching). Jeremiah's message brings threats to his life, physical beating, and near-fatal imprisonment in a slimy pit. Out of this suffering he pours out his feelings of anger, protest, and depression to God, and these are remarkably preserved in his book. We probably owe his book to his scribe, Baruch, who produced scrolls of Jeremiah's preaching (including the one that got burned, which he rewrote from scratch).

After the siege and destruction of Jerusalem in 588–587 BC (which he witnesses from inside), Jeremiah is freed by the Babylonians but then taken forcibly by a group of his own people who flee for safety to Egypt (against Jeremiah's advice; they refuse to listen to him right to the end). There, accompanied by his faithful friend Baruch, he dies. But his words live on, for they were vindicated by the events that unfolded just as he so horrifyingly had predicted.

While Jeremiah was the major prophet of seventh-century Judah, two other prophets of this era were Habakkuk and Zephaniah.

THE WIDER MESSAGE

This great swath of biblical history from Solomon to the exile, with its gallery of kings and prophets, has much to teach us. Here are three reflections.

Yahweh the God of Israel is in sovereign control of world history. The prophets assert that Yahweh is God, not merely of the tiny kingdoms of Israel and Judah but also of *all* nations *all* the time. Isaiah describes Assyria (the most fearsome world power of his day) as nothing more than a stick in the hand of God—a stick that will be discarded when it has served God's purpose. Jeremiah says the same thing about Babylon. Those who edited the historical books from Joshua to Kings did so during the exile when Israel was in captivity. Yet they continue to make the same affirmation of faith: Yahweh has done this. God is still in control, as he always has been. They would agree with how Revelation describes Jesus: "Ruler of the kings of the earth" (Revelation 1:5).

God demands justice, and politics matter to God. A
second vital truth that permeates this period is *the moral character and demand of Yahweh.* The God who acts for justice at
the exodus remains committed to maintaining it among his
own people. God not only assesses individual behavior but also
evaluates the moral health of society as a whole, from international treaties to market economies, from military strategy
to local court proceedings, from national politics to the local
harvest. Above all, God cares for those who are defenseless—
widows, orphans, the landless and homeless, immigrants and
refugees. Our fifth sentence does indeed express a central
theme in the prophetic books.

For that reason, God holds those who have political and economic authority in a nation especially accountable for their
policies and actions. The historical and prophetic books are full
of politics: economic policies, military strategies, judicial processes, public spending, infrastructure projects, taxation, diplomacy, international relationships, and so on. All of this comes
under God's gaze through the eyes and mouths of his prophets.
If the church is to be in any comparable way prophetic, then it
cannot avoid bringing the teaching of God's word into uncom-
fortable confrontation with political and economic realities of
our own contexts. And, like the prophets, we are unlikely to be
thanked for this message, and very likely to suffer.

***Outward religion without ethical transformation is abom-
inable to God.*** A third unmistakable message of this era is that
God does not want enthusiastic worship without practical social
justice. Or, as has been said, sacred rites do not compensate for
social wrongs. Even since the days of Samuel there had been the
awareness that "to obey is better than sacrifice" (1 Samuel 15:22).
But it is shocking when Amos and Isaiah tell the people that
Yahweh hates and despises their worship, and is fed up and

sickened by the very sacrifices they think he wants (Amos 5:21-24; Isaiah 1:11-16). God will not be worshiped and cannot be known apart from commitment to righteousness and justice, faithfulness and love, the things that define God's own character and are his delight (Jeremiah 9:23-24; 22:15-17).

Or, to return to our opening sentence from Micah, God has no need of lavish rituals. What he really wants is justice, compassion, and humility. Jesus agrees. All three of the above-mentioned prominent features of the message of the Old Testament in the period of the monarchy are found in the teaching of Jesus: God is king over all; submission to God's kingdom means radical ethical change; and practical obedience matters far more than religious observance. In these, as in so many ways, Jesus recaptures and amplifies the authentic voice of the Scriptures.

BACK TO THE COVENANT

God sends his prophets primarily to remind the Israelites of the covenant relationship that exists between them and to point out its implications. The prophets are recalling, reinforcing, explaining, and applying what the people should already know on the basis of all that God has done for them and said to them in the past, especially in those great events of the exodus and Mount Sinai that we explored in chapter three.

In simple terms, the covenant between Yahweh God and Israel involves three things.

1. There is a *history*. God acted to redeem Israel by delivering them out of slavery in Egypt. God also kept them safe in their wandering in the wilderness for a generation and then brought them into the land he promised. God has done so much for them, in his love and grace. That is the foundation of the law in the Torah and also the foundation for the message of the prophets.

2. There is a *commitment*. In the covenant, Yahweh God committed himself to be Israel's God, to bless and protect them, and to make them his instrument for bringing blessing to all nations. On the other side, Israel committed themselves to obey Yahweh's law and live as a whole society in the way God wanted, ultimately for their own good and as a model to the nations. That *mutual commitment* is at the heart of the relationship between God and Israel in the Old Testament.

3. There are *sanctions* (that is, promises and warnings). If Israel will live in God's ways and obey his law, then they will continue to enjoy God's blessing (not as a matter of earning or deserving it, but simply continuing in the place of blessing to which God, in his saving grace, has brought them). But if they will not, if they rebel, disobey, and go after other gods, then they will cut themselves off from his blessing and experience God's curse instead. In a world that is already under God's curse ever since the fall, Israel will be no different from the rest of the nations under God's judgment.

There are some great chapters in Leviticus and Deuteronomy that cover all three of these elements. They show how God's covenant includes history, commitments, and sanctions (promises and warnings). They also provide a very strong background for understanding the message of the prophets. Unless you love that armchair and have another very large cup of coffee, they are too long to read right now. But do plan to come back to them some time. They are: Leviticus 26; Deuteronomy 26; and Deuteronomy 28–30 (this last one gets pretty ghastly in the middle, but there's a happy ending in Deuteronomy 30).

Here at least is something of the flavor of them, condensed into a shorter passage that highlights especially the history and the commitments:

Ask now about the former days, long before your time, from the day God created human beings on the earth; ask from one end of the heavens to the other. Has anything so great as this ever happened, or has anything like it ever been heard of? Has any other people heard the voice of God speaking out of fire, as you have, and lived? Has any god ever tried to take for himself one nation out of another nation, by testings, by signs and wonders, by war, by a mighty hand and an outstretched arm, or by great and awesome deeds, like all the things the LORD your God did for you in Egypt before your very eyes?

You were shown these things so that you might know that the LORD is God; besides him there is no other. From heaven he made you hear his voice to discipline you. On earth he showed you his great fire, and you heard his words from out of the fire. Because he loved your ancestors and chose their descendants after them, he brought you out of Egypt by his Presence and his great strength, to drive out before you nations greater and stronger than you and to bring you into their land to give it to you for your inheritance, as it is today.

Acknowledge and take to heart this day that the LORD is God in heaven above and on the earth below. There is no other. Keep his decrees and commands, which I am giving you today, so that it may go well with you and your children after you and that you may live long in the land the LORD your God gives you for all time. (Deuteronomy 4:32-40)

With that background, in multiple ways the prophets essentially *remind* Israel of these things.

- *They remind Israel of their history.* God did so much for them in the past. But they are behaving now in a way that is utterly ungrateful and inconsistent. They are despising and betraying the relationship that God forged with them by his redeeming love and faithfulness.

- *They remind Israel of their commitments.* Israel promised to obey God but utterly failed to do so. In all kinds of ways, pointed out by the prophets, they have broken the covenant. This is often the most ruthless and shocking part of prophetic texts.

- *They remind Israel of God's threats and promises.* The covenant is very clear in warning them of the consequences of disobedience. Unless they change their ways, those consequences will happen. The curses of the covenant will fall on them. Thus the prophets warn the people by predicting the disaster lying ahead.

But the prophets can see beyond that disaster. They know that judgment will not be God's final word. The destruction of Jerusalem will not be the end for the people of God. God's promise to Abraham still stands, and God will always be faithful to that promise—since the salvation of the whole world depends on it. The prophets also bring a message of hope for the future, even in the face of disaster. They have good news to share. There is gospel in the Old Testament.

But for that, we must turn to the next chapter.

six

GOSPEL

> *How beautiful on the mountains are the*
> *feet of the One who brings good news.*
>
> Isaiah 52:7

There's nothing especially beautiful about feet.

But suppose you have been waiting in the ruins of a derelict city for two lifetimes (let's imagine), desperate for any fragment of good news, longing for any shard of hope. Suppose one day your straining eyes see a long-distance runner loping across the mountain ranges in the distance, bearing (your heart leaps to believe) good news. Then you would bless the feet that carry him toward you, and maybe even kiss them when he finally arrives and tells you between gasps for breath that God has won the victory, that salvation and peace have come, that "your God reigns!"

That is the scenario that Isaiah 52:7-10 places before our imagination. These verses may sound familiar, since several Christian hymns and songs have been based on them:

> How beautiful on the mountains
> are the feet of the one [the Hebrew word is singular]
> who brings good news,

who proclaims peace,
>who brings good tidings,
>who proclaims salvation,
who says to Zion,
>"Your God reigns!"
Listen! Your watchmen lift up their voices;
>together they shout for joy.
When the LORD returns to Zion,
>they will see it with their own eyes.
Burst into songs of joy together,
>you ruins of Jerusalem,
for the LORD has comforted his people,
>he has redeemed Jerusalem.
The LORD will lay bare his holy arm
>in the sight of all the nations,
and all the ends of the earth will see
>the salvation of our God. (NIV, with my change to
>>singular in verse 7)

Our sixth chapter sentence opens the dramatic sequence. Just as a movie director invites us to see things from his camera angle, so we are placed (in our imagination) in the burned-out ruins of Jerusalem, looking and longing for the day when Yahweh God, who allowed Nebuchadnezzar to destroy the city and even God's own temple back in 587 BC, will return home with his people. Two generations have passed. *Then a messenger comes running across the eastern hills with news*—and it is *good* news. God is coming back. The exiles are coming back home. The story of God's purpose through Israel for all nations to the ends of the earth will continue.

Now the phrase "brings good news" is a single word in Hebrew, and in the Greek translation of the Old Testament (known as the Septuagint) it is translated by the verb *euange-lizomai* (from which we get "evangelize"). This is a word we find frequently in the New Testament, with its noun, *euangelion* (in Latin, *evangelium*), meaning to proclaim *the gospel*—the good news that God has acted in Jesus of Nazareth to bring about all that prophets promised. That is exactly how Paul explains the Old Testament Scriptures in the synagogue in Pisidian Antioch. Here is the gospel, he says. This is the good news we are bringing to you. "We tell you the good news: What God promised our ancestors [that is, through the prophets] he has fulfilled for us, their children, by raising up Jesus" (Acts 13:32-33). In another place, Paul actually quotes our sixth sentence, referring to those who take the gospel to peoples who have not yet heard (Romans 10:15).

In this chapter we are thinking about the anticipation of the gospel in the Old Testament prophets. Some of them bring a message of incredible hope and joy, for all nations and for all creation. Their words were massively influential for how Paul understood what God had accomplished through Jesus and why that good news had to be shared with people of all the other nations (the Gentiles), not just the Jews. This provides the scriptural roots of the mission of the church to the nations.

However, as before, we have to set the message in the context of the story. The good news is highlighted by the bad news in the background, the very worst news, in fact, in the whole history of the Old Testament. Only when we feel the pain and despair can we see the beauty and hear the joy of our sixth sentence.

Exile in Babylon

Feel the terror of Israel's national trauma—the destruction of Jerusalem in 587 bc and the beginning of the exile in Babylon. Try to imagine the suffering of the people of Jerusalem during eighteen months of siege, starvation, and disease, ending with the final days of destruction, looting, and slaughter. Try to stumble with the exiles out of the burning city, screaming at the sight of the bloodshed around them amid the tormenting spears of Babylonian soldiers. Try to trudge with them, possibly in chains, across mile after mile around the Fertile Crescent and down into Mesopotamia (modern-day Iraq). Try to sit with them as strangers and captives in a foreign land, displaced, despised, and despairing. How do you feel? How do you react? How do you cope?

The people react. The Old Testament shows us that the Israelites react in several different ways to what has happened to them.

Some just turn their backs on Yahweh their God. It seems he was powerless or absent when they needed him most. They think things were better when they worshiped other gods (the very thing Jeremiah says brought judgment on them). They simply lose faith and go back to pagan practices (Jeremiah 44).

Others do accept that Yahweh has indeed brought judgment on them, but then respond to that perception in different ways. In the extreme horror of the suffering of Jerusalem, some protest that, even if the punishment was deserved (which they accept), was it not simply too appallingly vicious? How could God allow the Babylonians to inflict such cruelty—especially on women and children? The deeply moving poetry of Lamentations struggles with this, even while maintaining faith that God will not ultimately abandon them. Some cry out for vengeance on their enemies, particularly Edom and Babylon (Psalm 137). Others complain bitterly that, if this is God's judgment, then he is unfairly inflicting it on them when it is really all their parents' fault. They (the generation of the exile) are being made to suffer for the accumulated sin of their ancestors. Ezekiel has to address that distortion in Ezekiel 18; 33.

There is some truth in it: God was indeed patient for centuries with the sins of earlier generations. But that does *not* mean that the exile generation is *innocent*. They are suffering just judgment on their own sin. They are bearing the consequences of their own guilt.

Then there are some who accept that it is indeed Yahweh God's doing, and they have indeed deserved it. They refused to listen to his warnings through the prophets, and now the axe has fallen. Such people are completely broken in spirit. For them, the destruction of the temple and their expulsion from the land can mean only one thing: the covenant is shattered, and God has cast them off. They can see no hope. There is no more future for Israel. The end has come. They might as well be dead bones in a grave, as Ezekiel hears them saying (Ezekiel 37:11).

To this last group—those who nevertheless cry out to God in their desperation, pleading for his mercy and restoring grace (as in Psalm 74)—there will be words of hope, as we shall see. But first they need to *understand* clearly what has happened and why. That is the job of the prophets.

God gives future hope. The thing about God's judgment is not only that it is *logical* (within the covenant between God and Israel) but also that it is *limited.* As Leviticus 26 and Deuteronomy 28 make clear, God not only warned the people of the dangers of rebelling against him but also promised that beyond judgment lies the prospect of forgiveness and restoration. The whole relationship between God and Israel was founded on grace and it will continue by grace.

For that reason, many of the prophets bring promises of future blessing, even after the most fearsome preaching of judgment. Sometimes this comes right at the end of a prophet's book (as with Amos and Zephaniah). Sometimes it is inserted at key points on the way through (as with Hosea and Micah).

EZEKIEL

While Jeremiah was still in Jerusalem and reaching the end of his long prophetic ministry when Jerusalem fell, another younger prophet was in Babylon with the exiles and just beginning his life as a prophet: Ezekiel. Ten years before the rebellion that led to the destruction of Jerusalem in 587 BC, Nebuchadnezzar had made a punitive expedition against the city and taken some of its leaders into exile, including the then king, Jehoiachin. Among those first exiles in 597 BC was a young priest-in-training, Ezekiel, age twenty-five. Five years later, at the age of thirty, when he should be entering the priesthood in Jerusalem, God appears to him by a canal in Babylon and calls him to be a prophet. This is five years before Nebuchadnezzar's final attack. Jerusalem is still standing. Many of that first batch of exiles are deluded by false prophets into thinking that the city will never fall, and they will soon be on their way back home. Ezekiel knows otherwise and has the tough task of forcing them to face reality—the city *will* fall, and multitudes more will join them in exile. God's judgment is now inexorable.

Most of the prophets were rather unusual people, but Ezekiel is the strangest of them all. God inflicts a muteness on him, such that he is unable to speak except direct words of prophecy. This lasts five years until the day he receives news of the fall of Jerusalem, anticipated the previous day by the tragic death of his young wife, plunging him into grief that is in any case inexpressible. He engages in some very bizarre actions to act out his message. He lies down daily for a year and a half "besieging" a clay model of Jerusalem and eating starvation rations to portray the reality of the coming siege of Jerusalem. He shaves off his hair with a sword, then burns some, cuts some up, throws most of the rest to the wind, and saves only a few strands, again symbolizing the fate of the people. He experiences the most awesome visions of the glory of God. But in one of them, he is transported (in vision) back to the temple in Jerusalem and shown all the idolatries and wickedness that are happening there, as a result of which the glory of God is *departing* from the temple and Jerusalem. For a priest, that must have felt like the end of the world. Some of his speeches are shocking. Remember, he is not engaging in polite dialogue with academics. He is confronting a people who are brazenly refusing to accept what God says to them (brazen is right—God says they have foreheads of bronze). Ezekiel uses some of the most horrendous and frankly pornographic imagery to force them to feel what God feels about the ingratitude and promiscuous unfaithfulness of his covenant people.

After the news arrives that Jerusalem has indeed fallen (which vindicates both Ezekiel's and Jeremiah's messages), the second half of Ezekiel's book (from Ezekiel 33 on) has a different tone. He brings words of long-term comfort and hope to the people—just as Jeremiah did.

Sometimes it is concentrated in one place within the book, as in the following examples.

Jeremiah 30–33. These chapters are known as Jeremiah's Book of Consolation. The first two chapters are in poetry. They anticipate the judgment ahead but promise that it will not totally destroy the people. Though none of their allies will help them, God will ultimately come to their aid and restore their fortunes. There will be great reversal, and all the grief and mourning will be turned to joy. In Jeremiah 31:31-34, Jeremiah promises that God will make a new covenant with his people. It will have many similarities to the one he made with them after the exodus that they have so woefully broken, but it will involve a complete forgiveness of their sins. Jeremiah 32 records an incident in the life of Jeremiah that was a remarkable act of faith. Even though Jerusalem is besieged already and he is himself a prisoner of King Zedekiah, and even though he has no wife or children to be his heirs, Jeremiah buys a field, probably with the last few shekels he has. It is a sign of prophetic assurance that the people will return to their ancestral lands, long after Jeremiah's own death. Jeremiah 33 goes on to promise a future restoration of Israel with a son of David ruling over them in righteousness.

Ezekiel 34–48. The second half of Ezekiel contains amazing chapters of future hope. Ezekiel foresees a restoration of the kingdom of David (Ezekiel 34), the security of Israel's land and the cleansing of Israel's sin and shame (Ezekiel 36), a national resurrection and reunification (Ezekiel 37), the destruction of the enemies of God and God's people (Ezekiel 38–39), and the restoration of the worship of God in a renewed temple and a reconstitution of the whole people of God in a stylized allocation of the land and the presence of God in his city (Ezekiel 40–48).

Isaiah 40–55. By far the most glorious and sustained vision of future hope and blessing comes in these central chapters of the book of Isaiah. They are clearly addressed to the exiles, bringing assurance that God will act to bring them salvation. God will overthrow Babylon by the hand of Cyrus, the new and rising king of Persia, and then Cyrus will allow the Israelites to go back to their land. It is from these chapters of good news that our gospel sixth sentence comes.

If these chapters were originally spoken or written by Isaiah himself, the prophet who lived in Jerusalem in the eighth century (long before the Babylonian exile), then they must have been carefully preserved until the time when they could be relevant and revealed. Certainly they contain many phrases and themes that are common in Isaiah 1–39. Some prefer to think that these chapters are the preaching of a prophet whose name we don't know who brought this encouragement to the exiles near the end of their time in Babylon. This anonymous prophet (if he existed) was deeply influenced by the message of Isaiah, and so his prophecies have been attached to that book. Whichever view is right, it is the *content* of these Scriptures that matters more than the identity of who originally wrote them.

If you want a real spiritual tonic (in that armchair with the strong coffee), find some time to read right through Isaiah 40–55 in one sitting. Here are some of the great themes you will hear:

- A new future: The past is behind them. God's judgment is complete, and now God is on the move to do something new. It will be something greater than they have ever known. Make ready for God.

- A new exodus: God will lead them out of captivity in Babylon just as he led them out of slavery in Egypt. These chapters contain rich imagery about a new journey through the wilderness and how God will provide for them there. The language of redemption is strong.

- A new revelation of God: This new act of God will demonstrate that Yahweh alone is truly God, both creator of the universe and sovereign over history. He alone can predict events and interpret them afterwards through the words of his prophets. The gods of the nations, by contrast, are weak and powerless—indeed, they are nothing at all in comparison to the living God of Israel.

- A new hope for the nations: Like Israel, the other nations stand under God's judgment. But, also like Israel, they too can turn to God and find blessing and salvation. Isaiah 40–55 brings an explosion of color to the promise of God to Abraham. These chapters show how universal the faith of Israel actually is.

- A new figure to embody Israel: In the midst of Israel's failure, God reveals a new and mysterious person who will embody their identity and fulfill their mission: the Servant of the Lord.

THE SERVANT OF THE LORD

Israel itself is introduced as God's servant, chosen in Abraham to serve God's purpose (Isaiah 41:8-9). But they lamentably fail and end up (in exile) as a deaf, blind, and paralyzed servant (Isaiah 42:18-25). God then introduces a new figure as "my servant." He will share Israel's identity and carry forward Israel's mission, as the agent of God's blessing for the nations. Four particular passages have been called the Servant Songs: Isaiah 42:1-9; 49:1-6; 50:4-9; 52:13-53:12. Here are some of the features of this mysterious figure:

- He will be obedient to God in a way that Israel was meant to be.
- He will be filled with God's Spirit.
- He will carry out the justice of God among the nations.
- He will have the mission of bringing Israel back to God, and also bringing God's salvation to the ends of the earth as a "light to the nations."
- He will be a teacher, learning and passing on the word of God.
- He will suffer unjustly and be put to death.
- His death will be vicarious, that is, it will be not for his own wrongdoing but ours.
- Beyond death, he will triumph and see the fruit of his suffering.
- He will be exalted to the highest place.

Jesus was deeply influenced by these prophecies. He sees his own life, mission, death, and resurrection as fulfilling the role of the Servant of the Lord. The apostles go on to see that the mission of the Servant continues through the mission of the church to the Gentile nations (Acts 13:46-48).

THREE HORIZONS

We have spent a lot of time in this chapter and the last thinking about the message of the Old Testament prophets. Sometimes it can seem a little confusing. Especially when they do look into the future that God revealed to them, what do their words refer to? I find it helpful to think of three major possible horizons of their vision. That is to say, as the prophets launch their words into the future we can see three places where their words land, three places where their words are relevant and fulfilled—or still will be.

Horizon one: The Old Testament era. This is the horizon of the prophet's own time, or the wider Old Testament era as a whole. Most of what they predict happens either in their own lifetime or at some point within the history of Old Testament Israel.

For example, many prophets warn that God will send Israel, and then Judah, into exile because they persistently break the covenant and rebel against him. That is fulfilled, as we have seen, within the Old Testament period itself, in 721 BC for the Northern Kingdom of Israel, and in 587 BC for the Southern Kingdom of Judah. Those prophecies are fulfilled at horizon one.

Some of the prophets also predict that God will bring the exiles of Judah back to their land. He will bring their exile to an end. The covenant will be renewed, and they will rebuild the temple. Those prophecies are also fulfilled within the Old Testament period. After the edict of Cyrus, king of Persia, in 538 BC, several waves of exiles return to Jerusalem and the temple is rebuilt by 515 BC. Fulfillment at horizon one.

However, sometimes we will find that an Old Testament prediction that is made and fulfilled at horizon one can also carry forward and have even more significant fulfillment later. A good example is Isaiah's sign to Ahaz in Isaiah 7. Since it is a sign (something that is supposed to be meaningful for Ahaz), we have to assume that a child is indeed conceived and born soon afterwards, and that what Isaiah predicts about the defeat of Israel's enemies does indeed come true within approximately nine months—all at horizon one. God is indeed with them ("Immanuel") and delivers them from their enemies. However, we also know, of course, that Matthew finds an even greater level of fulfillment of that Immanuel prophecy in the birth of Jesus. That brings us to horizon two.

Horizon two: The New Testament era. There are some passages in the prophets that speak in terms that we now know could only ultimately be true in and through Jesus Christ and the gospel of salvation through his death and resurrection. Sometimes this is called messianic prophecy, though the word *messiah* (anointed one) itself does not often occur. The prophets do not only speak about a coming *person*, but rather they describe things that can only be perfectly true through Jesus. For example, when Jeremiah speaks about God making a new covenant (Jeremiah 31:31-33), much of what he says is *similar in principle* to the Sinai covenant. But when he says that part of this new relationship will include the complete forgiveness of sins, then we know that is accomplished only by Jesus Christ. Similarly, when Isaiah speaks about the Servant of the Lord, there are several things said about the Servant that are also said about Israel (chosen and loved by God, given as a light for the nations). But when Isaiah speaks about how the Servant will bear the sins of many and die vicariously for us (Isaiah 53), then we can only see such words fully embodied in the Lord Jesus. Thus we need to be alert to a possible gospel horizon in the words of the prophets. Please understand that this does not mean that we have to "find Jesus" in every verse of the prophets (or the Old Testament as a whole). Rather, it means we should be aware that these texts are all part of a great historical and scriptural journey that leads to Christ.

Horizon three: The new creation. There are times when prophets speak of a future that is described in terms that go way beyond anything we have experienced in the past or the present. For example, we know that the prophets speak about God judging Israel and also other foreign nations. But sometimes they describe God's judgment engulfing the whole earth and all nations in cataclysmic destruction of all that is wicked and evil (for example, Isaiah 24). Such a universal vision takes us to the ultimate horizon of the second coming of Christ and the final judgment.

Thankfully, however, the prophets more often have such long-term visions in relation to God's future blessing. Their words about the world of the future are filled with immense joy and excitement. We find ourselves imagining a world in which everything is perfect. Nature is full of abundance. The earth itself rejoices in its Creator. Human life is safe and fulfilling, and free from violence, injustice, hunger, and danger. War and violence are no more. People and animals live in harmony and peace. People never again turn away from God in disobedience. People from all over the world and all nations reject their false gods and turn to the living God and worship him with joy and gifts (for example, Isaiah 25:6-9; 35; 65:17-25; Jeremiah 32:37-41; 33:6-9; Joel 3:17-18).

That kind of vision is certainly not fulfilled at horizon one. The Israelites *do* return to their land (as we'll see in a moment). But they are still sinful and far from perfect—as books like Nehemiah, Ezra, and Malachi show. What about horizon two? Well, of course we know that Christ accomplished the redemption of the world in his death and resurrection, but we have not yet seen the fulfillment of all that the prophets describe, a world of perfect peace and justice. We have to take such passages on to the ultimate horizon three—or the eschatological horizon, to use technical terms.

By horizon three, I am referring to the picture of the new creation we see in Revelation 21–22. The whole scene in those chapters very deliberately echoes many of the themes in the prophets (the whole book of Revelation is saturated with Old Testament allusions). Read Isaiah 60 and 65:17-25 and then immediately read Revelation 21-22, and you'll see what I mean. Here are some comparisons:

	Isaiah	Revelation
New heaven and earth	65:17a	21:1
Former things gone	65:17b	21:4
No more weeping and tears	65:19b	21:4
No more death	65:20 (early)	21:4 (at all)
Jerusalem, city of God, a delight and joy	65:18b-19a	21:2
God present with and for his people	65:24	21:3
No more effects of the curse	65:22-23	22:3
No sun, for God will be the light	60:19-20	21:23, 22:5
The nations bring their gifts and glory into the city of God	60:5-6, 9	21:24-27

The ultimate vision of the prophets will only be fulfilled when Christ returns and the earth is cleansed and renewed to be the dwelling place of God with us.

There are some passages in the prophets that seem to include all three horizons, and this may feel confusing at first. But remember that the prophets are looking into a future that, as far as they can see, is all one single vision. They do not (could not) know that it will be centuries before horizon two comes along, and unknown centuries further before horizon three will come (it still lies ahead). *We*, with our perspective, can now see that their words have stretched out over a vast period of time. *They* saw things from the front, and saw things near and far as if they were all part of one big, single picture.

ISAIAH 52:7-10

The passage from which our chapter sentence comes, Isaiah 52:7-10, is a very good example of all three horizons. Take a look. Basically, this text is good news. That is what the running messenger of the beautiful feet announces. This is Old Testament gospel. It is good news at all three horizons.

Good news for the exiles: Horizon one. The messenger's words are to encourage the exiles to get ready to go home to Jerusalem. Yahweh has won the victory (God reigns), and God is already returning to his city and taking them with him. As at the exodus, God is redeeming his people. They can rejoice and go home. Indeed, that does happen. The prophecy is fulfilled at horizon one.

Good news in Christ: Horizon two. There are three aspects of the good news in these verses that are also true in Jesus Christ. Isaiah 52:7 speaks of the God who *reigns*. Isaiah 52:8 speaks of the God who *returns*. Isaiah 52:9 speaks of the God who *redeems*. All of those are true in Christ and the gospel. He preaches the kingdom of God. He goes to the temple (to which God promised to return). He is the Redeemer and Savior, through his death and resurrection. *Jesus* is God reigning, God returning, and God redeeming. Jesus adds a level of fulfillment to the messenger's words at the gospel horizon two.

Good news for the world: Horizon three. In Isaiah 52:10 the prophet moves to the global stage, to "all the nations" and "all the ends of the earth." This is the Abrahamic promise again. Through the mission of the church, the gospel of the salvation of our God is indeed going to the ends of the earth. The ultimate vision of the prophecy lies at horizon three. It will be finally fulfilled when the Lord Jesus Christ returns to reign over all the earth and to redeem his people from every tribe and people and language.

God's plan for the nations. Through all these horizons, there is a missional dimension to the prophets' vision of hope for the future. They see that, because God's promise to Abraham always envisaged God's blessing extending to all nations (as we saw in chapter two), there must come a day when people from other nations beyond Israel will be gathered in to be part of God's covenant people.

That is exactly what the apostle Paul realizes had to happen now that Messiah Jesus has come and fulfilled God's promised salvation through his death and resurrection. At the climax of Romans, as he prepares to use the church in Rome as his base for missionary work further west in Spain, he puts like this: "For I tell you that Christ has become a servant of the Jews on behalf of God's truth, so that the promises made to the patriarchs might be confirmed and, moreover, *that the Gentiles might glorify God for his mercy*" (Romans 15:8-9; my italics). Then he immediately supports that point with four quotations from the Old Testament. That is where the story has to go—to the nations—and Paul will take it there. The apostolic mission has its roots in the Old Testament.

We don't know what other scriptural texts Paul must have used in explaining his missionary commitment to take the good news to the Gentiles, but perhaps some like these, which envision people from many nations being registered in God's city (Psalm 87:3-6); coming to bring God worship (Psalm 86:8); being blessed with God's salvation, even as former enemies (Isaiah 19:20-25); being called by God's name (Amos 9:11-12); and being joined with God's people in Zion (Zechariah 2:10-11).[1]

Return from Exile

We have to come back, however, from such lofty future visions to the reality faced by the returning exiles in the closing centuries of the Old Testament.

As Jeremiah had said, Babylon's empire lasted about seventy years. Cyrus, king of Persia, defeated Babylon and launched a new era that would last another two hundred years, the Persian Empire. Cyrus's first act was an edict in 538 BC allowing captive peoples (peoples displaced by the Assyrians and Babylonians) to return to their native lands and take their gods with them. The Israelites, of course, believe that God has raised up Cyrus for this very purpose and for their benefit (Isaiah 44:24–45:6). The text of his edict, as it applies to the Israelites, appears in 2 Chronicles 36:23 (see also Ezra 1:1-4): "This is what Cyrus king of Persia says: 'The LORD, the God of heaven, has given me all the kingdoms of the earth and he has appointed me to build a temple for him at Jerusalem in Judah. Any of his people among you may go up, and may the LORD their God be with them.'"

Many (but far from all) of the Jews in Babylon do make the journey back in several waves over a number of years. They do not go back, however, to establish a new independent state of Judah or Israel. They become simply a tiny community within one corner of one of the provinces of the Persian Empire.

The returning exiles face a tough situation. The land has been neglected for nearly two generations. The city of Jerusalem is still a burned-out skeleton with no protective walls. The temple is gone. They face bad harvests and renewed problems of debt and taxation. On top of that, they face suspicion and opposition from the mixture of people in the northern part of the territory who pester them with threats and political slander against them to the Persian authorities. In short, it probably doesn't feel very much like the great poetic rhetoric of Isaiah 40–55.

The postexilic prophets. Into this depressing scene God sends several more prophets, the last of those who bring God's word to his people in the Old Testament period.

Haggai. Haggai's message is to encourage the people at a time of grief and depression. He begins by criticizing them for failing to complete the work of rebuilding the temple (their own houses seem to take higher priority) and urges them to finish the job. The people actually listen to him and do what he says. (He may have been quite surprised by this—it didn't happen to most of the prophets.) The temple (the one known to historians as the second temple) was completed and rededicated in 515 BC.

Zechariah. About the same time as Haggai (late sixth century BC), Zechariah also preaches to encourage. His messages are highly pictorial and symbolic, but their overall thrust is that God will restore Jerusalem (Zion) and destroy the enemies of his people. Zechariah portrays God sending his true king to Zion, but he will come riding on a donkey. No doubt Jesus had this prophecy of Zechariah in mind when he rode into Jerusalem a week before his death.

Malachi. Later than Haggai and Zechariah, probably in the mid-fifth century BC, Malachi sees that the priests and the people have become very lazy in their service of God. They seemed to feel that God does not care enough to help them very much, so why should they bother sacrificing the best of what they have to him? Such an attitude is robbing God, says Malachi. He warns them to change their ways before God himself will come to them. God will give plenty of warning of that day—he will send Elijah before God himself will arrive. That day was still more than four hundred years away when Malachi made that promise. But it is this last prophecy of Malachi (and of the whole Old Testament) that John the Baptist repeats, urging the people to repent and prepare for God's arrival. When Jesus told his disciples that John the Baptist *was* that Elijah who was to come, the real question immediately was, "Who then is Jesus?"

Ezra and Nehemiah. Another generation goes by. Persia is still the world empire. The temple has been rebuilt, but the people of Judah still live in difficult circumstances. Jerusalem is still partly in ruins and without walls. It is felt to be a disgrace to the God of the people who worship there. Those people are surrounded by non-Israelite population, and the danger of intermingling of religious practice and loss of identity is strong. There is a need for major reconstruction, not only of the physical walls of Jerusalem but also of the covenant faith and allegiance of the people.

Two men rise to the challenge in their own generation in the middle of the fifth century (that is, around 450 BC), Nehemiah and Ezra. They have both risen to high office within the Persian administrative service, living as they do among the Jews still resident in Mesopotamia. But at different times both of them are given official permission to go to Jerusalem with the king's authority to organize social, economic, and religious affairs there.

Nehemiah's great achievement is to rebuild the walls of Jerusalem in a short time and in the face of strong opposition from neighboring peoples. He brings the people together for this task, but he also calls them together for a renewal of their covenant with God after he discovers that some of the old problems of debt and poverty are fracturing the nation once again. He gives the people a renewed sense of identity and unity, even though they are a very small community. He has his successes, but even he recalls in his memoir that his greatest reforms easily fell into neglect.

Ezra was a priest and an expert in the law of Moses. By this time, the Pentateuch (the Torah, or first five books of the Bible) was probably in the form we now have them. We are told that he sets his heart to study, and to practice, and to teach the law of the Lord his God, a wonderful epitaph for anybody. He arranges a great ceremony that goes on for a week, reading God's Word to the assembled people and having some other trained priests explaining it as he goes along. He is concerned about Israelite men who have married foreign wives—not simply because of their foreignness (it is not a racial issue) but because of the danger of bringing idolatrous practice into the family lives of Israel. His solution is to insist that such men must divorce their foreign wives. Whether that is the right, or the only, thing to do is not explicit in the text, but it indicates how seriously he wants to preserve the purity of Israel's faith.

Waiting for God

Thus the period covered by the narrative and prophetic history of the Old Testament comes to an end. Another four centuries pass before the coming of the Messiah Jesus. During those years the people of Israel go through some very mixed times, sometimes at peace within a larger empire, but sometimes also going through times of intense persecution. Persecution happens especially when the Persian Empire is overturned by Alexander the Great and Judah becomes part of the subsequent Greek empires that follow, and then during the Roman Empire after that.

Two features of this so-called intertestamental period stand out. One is that the people of Judah, beginning with Ezra, became ever more committed to the book of the law. That is, they became a community founded and grounded in the Scriptures, and their life revolved increasingly around the demands and hopes of the Law and the Prophets. There were experts in the law (scribes and rabbis), and later a whole community of people seeking to live in perfect obedience to the whole law of God; they became known as Pharisees. The motives behind these movements were positive: if God punished Israel for disobedience to God's law, then if Israel is ever to find favor with

God again and avoid a repetition of such judgment, it must strive to ensure that everybody lives according to the law. The outcome, however, was to create a religious system that easily became overburdened with additional rules and protections—the system that Jesus challenged, to his cost.

The other feature of the period was an intensifying longing for God to intervene. As persecution increased, and as the wickedness and oppression of pagan nations that ruled over them went from bad to worse, it seemed that their only hope was for God to act directly and decisively to bring in his own kingdom. It felt like the exile had never really ended, even though they were back in their own land—back in the land but not yet free from evil empires. God must come. God must send the one he promised. God must establish his kingdom. God must liberate Israel and defeat his enemies. God must put an end to injustice and suffering.

Such were the hopes and longings of the people when a carpenter's son from Nazareth began preaching, "The time has come. The kingdom of God has come near. Repent and believe the good news!" (Mark 1:15).

seven

PSALMS AND WISDOM

The L*ord* *is my shepherd.*

P*salm* 23:1

O ur seventh and final sentence is possibly the most familiar word picture in the whole Old Testament. The Twenty-Third Psalm has inspired many hymns and songs, some of which are still regularly sung on occasions of great longing and trust in God's care and protection. It finds its place in the hope and joy of weddings. We pray these words also by the bedside of sick or dying loved ones. For those who have voices left to sing, the Twenty-Third Psalm lights a candle of trust amid the grief of a funeral, as we cling to the assurance of the final verse:

> Goodness and mercy all my life
> Shall surely follow me.
> And in God's house for evermore
> My dwelling-place shall be.

Rightly so. For it is indeed a song, a poem, composed (according to tradition) by the man who had himself been a shepherd boy and knew how to provide for the needs of his sheep. It speaks of God's care, protection, provision, and guidance for his people, one of many such songs in the book of Psalms. That book, standing at the center of our Bibles, has many other moods in its rich collection of the worship songs of Israel. We cannot get a grasp of the Old Testament without giving attention to the book of Psalms.

The book of Psalms comes in the third main section of the Old Testament, according to the order in the Hebrew canon: the Writings (the books that come after the Law and the Prophets). The other group of books in the Writings are known as the Wisdom literature—that is, Proverbs, Job, and Ecclesiastes. In this chapter we briefly survey both Psalms and Wisdom.

THE PSALMS

The book of Psalms is the edited collection of the songs of worship of Old Testament Israel, arranged in five books.[1] Like the hymns and songs in our Christian collections, these psalms have several different authors and emerge from many different circumstances. Together they express the whole faith of Israel (which was of course the faith of our Lord Jesus Christ, and our faith today), as it was lived out in the joys and pressures, wonders and struggles of everyday life.

The poetry. The Psalms, just like our hymns and worship songs, were written in poetry. Hebrew poetry doesn't use rhymes in the way a lot of English poetry does. The preference is for a kind of rhythmic pattern of repeating stresses (like three beats to the bar, and then another three, and so on). One very common feature of Hebrew poetry, known as parallelism, is the trick of saying more or less the same thing twice (in parallel lines, one after the other), but with minor variations so that it does not sound repetitive. Hebrew songwriters used this technique of parallelism as a way of filling out and emphasizing what they were saying or singing by giving it greater depth. The great thing is that, unlike rhyme, which is very difficult to reproduce in translation, parallelism is quite easy to recognize even in translation, as you can see just by looking at the Psalms in your English Bible.

There are several different kinds of parallelism. Here are some examples.

Repeating parallelism. The psalmist makes a point and then repeats it, using slightly different words and expanding the scope of what is being said. Essentially, the writer is making a single main point, even though he may spread it out over two or more lines. We need to connect the pieces together to get his full meaning.

> The heavens declare the glory of God;
>> the skies proclaim the work of his hands.
> Day after day they pour forth speech;
>> night after night they reveal knowledge. (Psalm 19:1-2)

In this example, the heavens and the skies are not proclaiming two separate things. No, the glory of God is seen in all the work of God's hands. They are not doing one thing by day and something else by night. No, the universe reveals truth about God *all the time.* The psalmist could have simply written, "Creation constantly reveals the glory of God," but the Hebrew poet gives it stereophonic depth and rhythm by his use of parallelism. This is probably the most common form of parallelism. Here's another example:

> Do not fret because of those who are evil
>> or be envious of those who do wrong;
> for like grass they will soon wither,
>> like green plants they will soon die away. (Psalm 37:1-2)

Contrasting parallelism. Sometimes the second line reinforces the first line by denying the opposite. The contrast makes the point all the more forcefully:

You have granted him [the king] his heart's desire
  and have not withheld the request of his lips. (Psalm 21:2)

I have kept the ways of the Lord;
  I am not guilty of turning from my God. (Psalm 18:21)

You save the humble
  but bring low those whose eyes are haughty. (Psalm 18:27)

Supplementing parallelism. Sometimes a second or third line builds on the first, adding significant further content. The parallel lines are not simply repeating the first line but substantially filling it out or adding a further dimension to it. Here are some examples:

Praise the Lord, my soul,
  and forget not all his benefits—
who forgives all your sin
  and heals all your diseases,
who redeems your life from the pit
  and crowns you with love and compassion.
      (Psalm 103:2-4)

For the word of the Lord is right and true;
  he is faithful in all he does.
The Lord loves righteousness and justice;
  the earth is full of his unfailing love. (Psalm 33:4-5)

These various forms of parallelism are also found in other poetic parts of the Bible, such as in the book of Proverbs and many of the messages of the prophets.

The metaphors. Like the prophets, the psalmists also like to use vivid mental pictures and comparisons. Often a single image can set the imagination racing. A strong metaphor can be more powerful than a thousand words. Take the Twenty-Third Psalm. David could have written many words about how God cared for him, guided him, protected him in trouble, and provided for his needs. Instead, he looked at the sheep he was guarding, and he said just two words (in Hebrew), "The LORD is my shepherd." With that simple picture David creates a whole world in our imagination (and gives us our seventh sentence).

That statement is, of course, a metaphor. It uses one reality (the life and work of a shepherd with his sheep) to describe another reality (the way God cares for people). The second of those realities is what the poet is actually talking about (the *target* of the metaphor). The first is the one he is using for comparison (the *source* of the metaphor). The Psalms are bursting with metaphors like this.

Some metaphors are pictures to help us imagine God. God is a rock, a shield, a fortress, a strong tower, a roaring lion, a chariot rider, an archer, a light, a father, a king, a builder, a shepherd. God is pictured with eyes, ears, hands, feet, and a very loud voice. Of course, God is not *literally* any of these. But each of them is a metaphor that speaks powerfully and imaginatively about God. They convey truth in a way that abstract descriptions can't quite match.

Some metaphors picture different human experiences. Psalmists speak of sinking in mud or being washed away in a flood. They feel surrounded by wild beasts or pinned to the ground. They can compare themselves to a wineskin dried up in the smoke or a worm in the earth. Or they can frolic like calves or have their horns lifted high like a champion bull. They may be standing on a rock or hiding under the wings of a large bird. They can flourish like a palm tree or trample on lions and snakes. All of these, of course, are pictures that speak of different kinds of experiences.

We need to let such rich poetic metaphors do their work in our minds and imagination. We have to ask, "What are they telling us about God or about life?" But we should not reduce them to bald factual statements. Let them fly (metaphorically speaking).

The emotions. The range of experiences and feelings in the book of Psalms is simply vast. Drop into the Psalms almost anywhere, and very soon you will come across examples of all of these: joy and happiness, gratitude and thanksgiving, awe and wonder, pain and hurt, anger and bitterness, remorse and sorrow, puzzled questioning, longing, agony, hope, trust, and relief.

Such emotions arise from a wide range of experiences and situations that people can find themselves in. The psalmists can speak in different ways about experiences such as these: being alone; being with others; being falsely accused; being in acute danger or distress; being seriously ill, even close to death; suffering loss or injury; being rescued from danger; feeling guilty for doing something sinful; being thankful for God's gifts or actions; traveling to worship God in Jerusalem; going into battle; coming back from battle; giving testimony in public worship; seeing their city and temple destroyed; going into exile and longing for home.

Originally, of course, these songs were written by people and addressed to God. They are *human* words spoken (mostly) *to God*. Yet now we read them in the Bible, and so they function as *God's word to us*. The Psalms have become part of God's message to us, not just human words to God. I think this is because of the way God himself is so deeply involved in the experiences and the emotions that fill the Psalms. God was right there in those situations that the psalmists faced. When they eventually collected the Psalms for later generations of Israelites to sing, they recognized that *God could continue to speak* to his people again and again through the words of the original writers and the circumstances they faced. In the same way, through reading and singing these songs, *God also speaks* to all of us when we face similar situations and have similar emotions.

The variety. Just like the hymns and songs we sing, there are different kinds of psalms suitable for different occasions. Here are some of the different categories.

Hymns of praise.[2] The shortest psalm (Psalm 117) gives us a perfect example of the key elements in such hymns of praise.

> Praise the LORD, all you nations;
>> extol him, all you peoples.
> For great is his love toward us,
>> and the faithfulness of the LORD endures forever.
> Praise the LORD.

The usual structure is

1. *A summons to praise.* It may be short or expanded, or sometimes just assumed.

2. *The reasons for praise.* Often this is introduced by the word *for*. All kinds of reasons are given in hymns of praise, but usually they either describe what God is like (his greatness, character, goodness, faithfulness, and so on) or declare what God has done (his great acts in creation and redemption, or both).

3. *A renewed call to praise.* This again may be short (just a quick "Hallelujah" to finish off), or more extended and reflective. Sometimes it may lead to a call to trust God, for the same reasons that we were called to praise him.

Psalm 33 is a good example. It begins with a call to praise (Psalm 33:1-3), and it ends with an affirmation of trust and hope (Psalm 33:20-22). In between it gives reasons for praise and foundations for hope. That is a classic hymn of praise.

Thanksgivings.[3] Thanksgiving is also part of praise, of course, but it focuses on some particular thing that God has done in the experience of the author of the psalm or for the people he wants to sing with him. Most thanksgiving psalms were written by individuals, referring to some act of God for which they were thankful. This may be for deliverance from enemies or illness or death, victory in battle, or forgiveness of sins. Some are community thanksgivings when the whole people give thanks to God for a good harvest or for deliverance from enemies (for example, Psalms 65; 124).

Laments and protest songs. Lament psalms also have a typical structure. It goes rather like this:

God, I'm suffering pretty badly here.

God, everybody is against me, or laughing at me. It's horrible and it isn't fair.

God, you aren't doing anything to help right now, and I desperately need you to.

How long will this go on, please? Must I wait forever?

But God, I still trust you and will go on praising you, no matter what.

That last element is found in most of the psalms of lament. There is a shift from the misery and pain of the lament to some expression of hope, trust, or the expectation of deliverance and renewed praise. Occasionally, though, the lament lasts right to the end of a psalm, and the psalmist seems to find no comfort at all. That is true in Psalm 88, which is probably the darkest of all the psalms of lament—indeed, it ends in darkness. I'm sure it speaks for many down the ages who have found no end to their sufferings, at least in this life.

About two-thirds of the Psalms include some lament, and a few are almost nothing but lament. These are songs of protest, songs in distress, songs out of suffering and pain. Many of them are individual laments, while others are community laments sung by the whole people in moments of terrible distress.[4]

Here's a surprising little fact. The title of the whole book in Hebrew is "The Praises." Yet the largest group of "praises" are actually *laments*. This may seem contradictory to us, but that is because we usually think of praise only as something we do when we feel happy and joyful. But for Israel, praise was something far deeper than that. Praise could happen even in the darkest moments—in fact, especially in those darkest moments.

For Israel, praising God meant *recognizing God's reality and presence*. Praise meant affirming that the Lord God of Israel is the one and only true and living God. Praise described the *character* of God and declared the *acts* of God. Praise is to bow down in God's presence (no matter what the circumstances) and affirm, "God is alive, and God is here, and God has said this and done that."

Then, crucially, praise meant bringing the whole of life into the presence of God in that same way. Not just the nice bits of life for which we want to say, "Thank you very much," but also all the tough and baffling bits of life, about which we want to cry out, "What's going on here?" The psalmists brought the whole of themselves into the whole of what they knew about God. When life was painful, or unbearable, or simply beyond understanding—they threw all that up to God and cried out to him. Notice that they cried out *to* God. They did not cry out *about* God to other people, as we so often do with our complaints. No, they brought it all into the presence of God and stood there, or kneeled there, weeping, wondering, waiting.

I think we have lost something in Christian worship because we hardly ever allow ourselves or others to do this. We ignore the psalms of lament. Instead we try to pretend that everybody is, or should be, happy. We even imply (or actually say) that if you are not happy and joyful in your worship, there is something wrong with you or with your faith. We do not encourage or allow people to be *honest* in worship and truly engage with God in the midst of their struggles. The Psalms do exactly that, and so should we.

There are several other kinds of psalms in the book, such as these:

- psalms of Zion (about Jerusalem and the temple there as the heart of Israel's worship, and also describing Zion as symbolic of the people of God themselves)[5]

- psalms of pilgrimage (sung by those going up to Jerusalem to worship)[6]

- royal psalms (about the kings in the line of David, or sometimes also celebrating the kingship of Yahweh, the God of Israel over all the earth)[7]

The message. Having gotten our heads around the nature of the book, what is it there for? What do the Psalms *do* in the minds and lives of God's people? The Psalms did for Israel what they can still do for us as Christians, within the context of all the additional songs and liturgies of our worship. Worship that regularly draws on the resources of the Psalms does at least three things: it generates and strengthens faith, it challenges us in how we live in the world, and it inspires us with hope (this is why, speaking personally, I so much regret the almost total neglect of the Psalms in many Christian churches today).

Faith. The book of Psalms is a remarkable affirmation of all the great contours of biblical faith—about God, creation, sin, salvation, God's people, personal and community holiness, and future hope for the world and the nations. Remember those seven acts of the drama of Scripture that we surveyed in the introduction? There are Psalms that connect in some way with each of them:

- There is praise for God as Creator and outpouring of joy in creation.

- The realities of sin and evil are exposed in lurid colors.

- The promises of God to Israel are celebrated and their Old Testament history remembered, with joy or regret.

- The coming of the kingdom of God in the person of Jesus is anticipated in some of the royal psalms, where the language about the Davidic king goes way beyond Old Testament historical reality.

- Some psalms envisage the good news of God's name and salvation going to all nations in all the earth—a vision that inspired the Gentile mission of the New Testament church and still inspires us today.

- Some psalms look forward eagerly to the day when all people and all creation will rejoice in the just judgment and salvation of God.

The Psalms not only declare the faith of God's people. They also serve to strengthen and sustain faith in tough times. Many psalms are calls for trust in God in spite of great suffering, or encouragement to wait for God to do what he has promised, in confidence that he will do so, even if it seems to take a long time: "How long, O Lord?" Don't stop trusting. Some of the psalms are very painful, because they express this longing for God to act, to stop evil people doing such evil things, and to rescue those who are suffering. They may not seem very relevant to Christians living in comfort and freedom, but they are very precious and profoundly meaningful for Christians living under persecution or in the midst of wars, destruction, and loss. We can pray such psalms on their behalf.

Hope. Many psalms express such longing and hope at an individual level. But there are also some psalms that affirm an even wider hope: the universal vision of all nations in all the earth coming to know and worship the living God and rejoice in his salvation. Here's just one example:

All the nations you have made
   will come and worship before you, Lord;
   they will bring glory to your name. (Psalm 86:9; my italics)

There are a whole lot more. Can you feel the surging hope and expectation for God's whole world throbbing in such verses? Psalms 22:27; 47:1; 67:3-5; 72:17; 96:1-3, 10-13; 102:15; 117:1-2; 138:4-5. Don't they fill a vast horizon of faith imagination? I often wonder what went on in the minds of Israelites singing such words. How did they imagine such things could ever happen?

Yet clearly the Israelites who wrote and sang such songs *did* have the imagination to believe that God would somehow make the vision a reality. Paul refers this as the mystery hidden for ages (Colossians 1:26). That is, the Old Testament Israelites believed that God would one day keep his promise to Abraham (which is echoed in several psalms) in such a way that people from all nations would be so blessed by God that they would come to worship him. But the mystery, what the Israelites could not have known, was *how* God would do that. Now, of course, we do know. For, as Paul says, the mystery has now been revealed *through the gospel* (Ephesians 2:11–3:6). It is *through the Lord Jesus Christ* that the way has been opened for people of all nations to come to God. Paul quotes Psalm 117 among a number of the Old Testament texts that celebrate in advance the missionary expansion of the church among the Gentile nations (Romans 15:11). The Psalms anticipate that great vision and hope, and call us to trust in its ultimate completion.

Life. Psalm 1 has clearly been placed right there as a preface to the whole book of Psalms. It alerts us, before we plunge into the songs that follow, that worship is not just about how well we can sing but about how well we are living.

The righteous person delights in and meditates on "the law of the LORD" (Psalm 1:2).[8] These two words (*delights* and *meditates*) do not mean that the psalmist was involved in some merely emotional or intellectual activity. Rather this person *loved* God's law and was *living* God's law—putting it into practice. This psalm, at the very head of the whole book, shouts out a blessing on those who live their faith in God by following God's instructions. That is the only kind of person who can worship God acceptably (as Psalms 15; 24 explain further).

What's more, clearly this "blessed" one does not see the law as a stern, heavy burden of requirements that one must legalistically carry out to the letter. One *delights* in the Torah. One's life is fruitful because of it. This is not a code of religious slavery but a recipe for responsible freedom and joy in living life in the presence of the living God. Psalms 19; 119 make the same point repeatedly: those who live their lives in joyful obedience to God's ways find all kinds of benefits through God's blessing.

Even in those psalms that are simply praising God, there are lessons for life. For Israel, the character of the Lord their God was their best clue as to how God wanted them to live their own lives. Whenever they sang songs praising the Lord because he is faithful, truthful, trustworthy, just, compassionate, loving, caring, or providing—the unspoken but very powerful implication was, "*That* is what *we* ought to be like also." Worship motivates us to become like the one whom we worship. Worship, if it reflects the great truths of the Psalms, is life shaping.

When the people of Israel worshiped God regularly using the Psalms, they were learning all the time. Not just learning in the head, but *learning for living.* Many psalms offer reflections about life, wisdom for times of trouble, good advice for living in a way that pleases God. Above all, they give constant encouragement to go on trusting God and walking in God's way, even when the ways of the wicked seem more enticing. Sometimes these are called wisdom psalms, because they are similar in some ways to what we find in the Wisdom literature.[9]

Thus, finally, we turn to those books in which such lessons for living were collected.

Wisdom Books

One day a bunch of people felt angry enough with what the prophet Jeremiah was telling the nation that they decided to get rid of him for good. Their reasoning is revealing. In short, what they say is, "One less prophet won't make any difference. We will still have all the teaching and preaching we need." Here's exactly what they say: "Come, let's make plans against Jeremiah: for the teaching of the law by the *priest* will not cease, nor will counsel from the *wise*, nor the word from the *prophets*" (Jeremiah 18:18; my italics).

They clearly recognize three groups of what we might call professionals in the community: the experts in the law (priests), those who bring a direct word from God (prophets), and a third group, "the wise." This was a class of people, well-known also in other nations surrounding Old Testament Israel, renowned for their knowledge and wisdom. People consulted them for advice on matters great and small—affairs of state, or family discipline. Some were government advisers. Maybe our modern word for them would be *consultants* (though they probably got more respect than so-called consultants tend to have in our culture).

Thus, as well as the books of the Law (the Torah) and the books of the Prophets, we have books in our Old Testament that emerged from this community. They come in the third section of the Hebrew canon, the Writings, which also includes the book of Psalms. Three books are regarded as Wisdom literature: Proverbs, Job, and Ecclesiastes.

A distinctive voice. We need to read these books knowing that we are listening to a different kind of voice from other texts.

Here are some of the differences between the Wisdom books and other parts of the Old Testament.

Not laws. Biblical laws are usually short and imperative. They tell you what you must do, or must not do, and sometimes state a penalty for breaking them. The Wisdom voice makes the same point, but often in a more conversational way. With an arm around your shoulder, it invites you to think about the consequences of certain behaviors, to think twice about the company you keep, and to avoid getting entangled with shady men or seductive women or both.

For example, compare the laws on adultery in Exodus 20:14, Leviticus 20:10, and Deuteronomy 22:22, with the advice and warnings of Proverbs 5; 6:20-25. The style is very different. The laws are blunt and to the point. "Don't do it! The penalty is death if you do." It is a straight command from God, backed up by a severe legal penalty. Proverbs is not so much a command as a strong warning backed up by pointing out some of the disastrous results: "It can ruin yourself and your family. You have far too much to lose. Think again!"

As well as such lengthy advice, the book of Proverbs contains hundreds of shorter statements. It is important to remember that *proverbs are not laws.* They are not absolute commands, or rules, or predictions of what will always happen. They are short, pithy statements about all kinds of situations in life. They offer insights and perspectives and guidelines, not hard-and-fast rules. They tell us that certain kinds of behavior will usually produce good results, and the opposite kinds of behavior will usually produce bad results. Wise people choose the first. Foolish people choose the second. The results *usually* follow. But we can't turn these general observations either into unalterable laws or into guaranteed promises. Life is more complicated than that. Things don't always work out in the way proverbs state so simply.

The Wisdom writers knew that, which is why we have the books of Ecclesiastes and Job.

Not prophets. When the Old Testament prophets speak about issues of life, society, politics, economics and religion, they are very confrontational. They address people directly, sometimes naming names. They focus on very particular matters in their own historical context, often with words of specific condemnation of people and practices that are flouting God's law. They summon people to respond—to repent and change their ways.

The Wisdom writers are much more broad brush in what they say about public life. They state principles and expectations, laying out the ideals of good government and healthy economic activity in general terms. Read, for example, Proverbs 8:12-16 (see also Proverbs 16:10, 12-13; 20:8, 26; 25:2-5; 31:1-9).

> I, wisdom, dwell together with prudence;
>> I possess knowledge and discretion.
> To fear the LORD is to hate evil;
>> I hate pride and arrogance,
>> evil behavior and perverse speech.
> Counsel and sound judgment are mine;
>> I have insight, I have power.
> By me kings reign
>> and rulers issue decrees that are just;
> by me princes govern,
>> and nobles—all who rule on earth. (Proverbs 8:12-16)

Once again, there is no conflict in principle between the prophets and the wise, but there is a different tone of voice. Proverbs describes what ought to be, while the prophets describe what actually is—the situation on the ground, as we say. We need both perspectives. You can't criticize the way things are unless you have some vision of the way things ought to be. The Bible gives us both.

Not history. As we saw in earlier chapters, both the Law and the Prophets point back to the history of Israel. They remind Israel of the exodus. They remind Israel of the covenant. They tell Israel that, because of their history, they should know how to live in a way that is consistent with what God has so graciously done for them. Take a look at these laws—they all use the history of redemption (the exodus) as motivation for doing what God commands in relation to the poor and oppressed: Exodus 23:9; Leviticus 19:33-36; 25:39-43; Deuteronomy 15:12-15; 24:14-22. As an example, look at the first one on the list: "Do not oppress a foreigner; you yourselves know how it feels to be foreigners, because you were foreigners in Egypt" (Exodus 23:9).

The Wisdom writers, by contrast, do not refer to the history of Israel at all. They don't make any explicit use of the great historical traditions of Israel's faith—the promise to Abraham, the exodus, Moses, the Sinai covenant, the wilderness wanderings, the conquest of the land, and so on. They don't refer to that story of redemption that we know so well from the early books of the Bible. *Yet they must have known those great traditions*—they were Israelites. They are just as concerned as the Law and the Prophets about ethical issues such as helping the poor and needy.

How *do* they motivate their exhortations? By going even further back, *to creation itself.* They know that the same God who was the redeemer of Israel is also the Creator of the world and all nations. They know that all human beings are equally created in the image of God. They reckon that if God is morally consistent, then God's standards should apply to all people. They see that there are moral principles built into creation itself. There are ways of living that are good for people anywhere, and other ways of living that will be damaging for human life everywhere. In other words, while the Law and the Prophets are addressed to *Israel in particular as God's redeemed people*, Wisdom literature has a more universal human appeal. Here are some examples of this wider, creational appeal: Proverbs 14:31; 17:5; 19:17; 22:2; 29:7, 13. As one other example, let's look at Job 31:13-15.

> If I have denied justice to any of my servants,
>   whether male or female,
>   when they had a grievance against me,
> what will I do when God confronts me?
>   What will I answer when called to account?
> Did not he who made me in the womb make them?
>   Did not the same one form us both within our mothers?

This is a remarkable insight and affirmation—that a master and slave are human beings, both born of human mothers, both made and formed by the one Creator God. That note of created quality is unique in comparison with the slave laws and customs of the peoples surrounding Israel.

This creational appeal fits in very well with what we saw in earlier chapters about Israel's role in God's plans for the whole world. God created Israel from the very beginning to be the means of blessing the nations. God gave them his law partly in order to shape them to be a model for the nations. The teaching that we find in Old Testament law could be used as an example or paradigm for others. That is what the Wisdom writers do. They see the general principles embodied in Israel's history and laws, and they turn them into advice, guidance, proverbs, and pictures that can be understood and taken to heart by anybody.

A positive voice. The book of Proverbs is a broadly positive and optimistic compendium of wisdom and advice. It holds up before us the ideals of a life that is lived in a way that is wise, godly, and righteous. That is to say, it binds together things that we sometimes separate out—the intellectual and religious and ethical realms of life. Two opposite character equations, connecting all three of these dimensions, run like contrasting threads through the book:

Wise = godly = righteous
Foolish = ungodly = wicked

This in turn makes it clear that wisdom and folly, as descriptions of human beings, are not just intellectual qualities, to do with being very learned and academically bright, or simply stupid and dim. On the contrary, very clever people can do very foolish and wicked things. In Proverbs, wisdom and folly are *moral and spiritual* categories, reflecting how we live in relation to God and God's ways.

The book repeats, like a kind of motto, "The fear of the LORD is the beginning of knowledge."[10] That means that putting God first as the one whom we love, worship, trust, and obey is not just the *starting point* of wise living (something you can leave behind when you grow up), but it also remains the *first principle* of sensible and ethical living—a guiding principle for the whole of life.

From that perspective, the book of Proverbs surveys many areas of life and offers principles for good and successful living: in relationships between husbands and wives, parents and children, in the world of work and business, in social and political life, in the economic realities of wealth and poverty, in the use of our tongues (for good or ill), in our friendships, in eating and drinking, and so on. The overall message is: trust in God and live like this, and things will (or should) turn out well for you and your family. That is sound advice. That's how life works best.

Most of the time.

A questioning voice. But not all the time. Indeed, for some people life never, or hardly ever, works out the way it is supposed to by conventional wisdom. The wisdom writers knew this perfectly well. That is why we have not only the book of Proverbs but also the balancing and contrasting books of Job and Ecclesiastes.

The book of Job wrestles with the problem of the suffering of good people who don't seem to deserve it. It is a brilliantly written drama in which we see a man who is as righteous as can possibly be imagined (both the narrator and God himself say so; Job 1:1, 8; 2:3) suffer the worst calamities than can be imagined (loss of property, family and health—one disaster after another). The speeches of his friends explore all the possible reasons for his suffering, especially the theological reason that he must be suffering because of sins he has committed. This, after all, is what the Bible says—sinners will suffer, so Job must have sinned terribly.

But they are completely wrong. We know it (because we've read the opening chapters of the book of Job), God knows it, and Job knows it. Still he suffers. The worst of it is not just his suffering but the *silence of God*. Job cannot get through to God in order to state his case and be vindicated. In the end, when God speaks, God does not answer the problem of suffering (as we all wish he would). Rather, God restores his relationship with Job and in effect asks him to trust the God who is greater than we can begin to imagine, the God who ultimately controls the very forces of evil that we don't understand. In those great speeches at the end of the book, God seems to be saying, "If you don't know and can't imagine how I created and manage this physical world you see all around you, don't think you can fathom my governance of the moral universe. My ways are beyond you, but you can trust me."

The book of Ecclesiastes wrestles with the problem of how futile life seems. The author knows that life is full of good things—food and drink, work, marriage, family, and so on—and that these things are indeed good gifts from God that we should enjoy. But so often even the best things in life end up destroyed or wasted, or going to the wrong people. In the end death seems to make it all pointless anyway. The writer knows it is better to be wise than to be a fool, but when you're dead, what does it matter? A dead wise man is just as dead as a dead fool, and both are as dead as a dead dog. What's the difference in the end? It's all meaningless, frustrating, pointless, enigmatic, and baffling (those are some of the flavors of the Hebrew word that used to be translated as "vanity").

The author of Ecclesiastes was not an atheist. In fact, he repeatedly affirms that God is in charge of the world, and he goes on trusting in God and telling others to do so, but he is simply *baffled*, grieved, and depressed by what happens in our world. Aren't we all, sometimes? We are confronted with the terrible chasm between the givenness and goodness of creation, life, and work (the world of Genesis 1–2), and the catastrophic consequences of the fall in Genesis 3. We live in a world of tension between both realities.

The books of Job and Ecclesiastes *give us permission* to question, struggle, and protest (just like the psalms of lament). It is actually a great relief and encouragement that God chose to include these books within the great library of our Bible.

But exactly at that point, we remember that we *do* have the rest of the Bible. We must read a book like Ecclesiastes in the light of the whole Bible. For while it does speak the truth, it is not the *whole* truth, and that difference really matters. The writer of Ecclesiastes could not know what we now know through the New Testament. He did not know that God (whom he trusted but couldn't understand) would one day enter this world himself. In the incarnation of his Son, God experienced all the limitations and frustrations of life in this crazy world. Then God himself, in Christ, suffered exactly what one verse in Ecclesiastes describes as something meaningless, and God turned it into the means of our salvation.

There is something else meaningless that occurs on earth: *the righteous who get what the wicked deserve, and the wicked who get what the righteous deserve* (Ecclesiastes 8:14; my italics).

Exactly that first thing happened to Jesus on the cross. But God raised him from the dead. That is God's answer to the apparent futility of death. God has conquered it in Christ's resurrection. For that reason, our life and work is "not in vain" in the Lord (1 Corinthians 15:58). The gospel of the life, death, and resurrection of Jesus is the Bible's own answer to the challenge of Ecclesiastes.

Once again, I hope you can see how much it helps when we set everything we read in the Bible within the flow of its great story. The Bible *as a whole* brings us God's good news. Even when we read the bad-news parts, we can make sense of them in light of God's fullest revelation in the gospel. Even a book like Ecclesiastes with its unanswered questions and unfulfilled longing is pointing us forward to the Christ in whom the whole Old Testament finds its ultimate fulfillment.

That brings us to the end of our seven sentences. I don't know whether the apostle Paul would approve of my choice of these seven, but I hope he would recognize the same basic journey though the Scriptures that he traces again and again: creation, Abraham, exodus, David, the prophets, the Psalms. Like Paul, we have seen that this is a journey that ultimately leads to Jesus of Nazareth, Messiah of Israel, Savior, and Lord of the nations. For after all, what we call the Old Testament was the Bible of Jesus. These were the stories he knew. These were the songs he sang, the scrolls he heard read, and the prayers he prayed every Sabbath. These were the prophetic texts in which he discerned the shape of his own identity and mission. This was the people to whom he belonged. This was the God he knew as Abba, Father. For us, the more we get to know the Scriptures of the Old Testament, the closer we will come to the mind and heart of Jesus himself.

DISCUSSION QUESTIONS

Chapter 1: Creation

1. How would you define a worldview? How does the book define it?

2. What does it mean that creation is distinct from but dependent on God?

3. What makes humans special or unique? What messages do you hear from our culture about the difference between humans and other living beings?

4. Do you tend to think of sin as something that affects individuals or groups of people? How have you seen sin affect society as a whole or generations of people?

5. What is the solution that God provides for sin?

Chapter 2: Abraham

1. In what ways is Genesis 12 the restart of the story?

2. What are the three particular promises God makes to Abraham?

3. What does "blessing" mean in the context of this promise?

4. What is the goal or purpose of this promise to Abraham?

5. Describe Abraham's relationship with God. In what ways is it similar to your own relationship with God? In what ways is it different?

6. In what ways does God's promise of blessing for all nations affect your biblical understanding of God's mission and your part in it?

CHAPTER 3: EXODUS

1. How does this chapter's sentence serve as a foundation for the Ten Commandments? Why does it matter that this sentence comes before the first command?

2. Where do we see redemption in this chapter? What has redemption meant in your own life? How does a biblical understanding of redemption affect the way you see the world around you?

3. Describe God's covenant with the people through Moses. What did it include?

4. How is Deuteronomy like an ancient Near Eastern treaty? Does this parallel surprise you? Why or why not?

5. Where do we see grace in the law? How is the law related to mission? What does "keeping the law" or "failing to keep the law" mean for us now as believers in Christ?

CHAPTER 4: DAVID

1. What is the link that Paul makes between David and Jesus?

2. How do you understand the conquest of the Canaanites? What stood out to you in the conversation on genocide?

3. How do we see God at work through the period of the judges? What is the cycle of action? Can you think of times in your own life when you went through cycles of rebellion and repentance?

4. How did Israel end up as a monarchy? Why do you think the people wanted a king? How do you see the relationship between human desires and God's sovereignty?

5. What are God's promises to David? How do we see a connection between these promises and Jesus?

CHAPTER 5: PROPHETS

1. What was the job of the prophets? Was it to predict the future? Explain the difference between foretelling and forthtelling.

2. What methods did the prophets use to get their message across? Do you find yourself resonating with a particular method of persuasion? Do you tend to use one of these methods when you want to be heard?

3. What are some of core themes of the prophets' messages? In what ways do we need these same messages today?

4. What are the goals of the prophets?

CHAPTER 6: GOSPEL

1. If you tried to imagine the suffering of the people of Israel in exile, how did it feel?

2. How did the people react to the exile? How can you relate these feelings and reactions to Christians in the world today who are experiencing persecution and displacement and exile?

3. Read through Isaiah 40–55. What important insights do you see about God and his action in the world?

4. What are the three horizons of prophetic fulfillment? Does this concept help you to understand the prophets more? Suggest other prophetic texts that could illustrate the different horizons.

CHAPTER 7: PSALMS AND WISDOM

1. What are some ways that Hebrew poetry differs from English poetry?

2. What do the psalms of lament show you about God? What about the psalms of praise?

3. Do you read the psalms in worship? In private prayer? How have they been helpful to your faith journey?

4. How do the wisdom books differ from the law, the prophets, and historical books?

5. What is the purpose of the wisdom books? In what ways could you or your church make better use of them in evangelism, discipling, preaching, etc.?

NOTES

INTRODUCTION

[1]This idea as a way of laying out the story and message of the whole Bible comes from Craig G. Bartholomew and Michael W. Goheen, *The Drama of Scripture: Finding Our Place in the Biblical Story*, 2nd ed. (Grand Rapids: Baker, 2014). They propose a six act sequence in the Biblical drama by including the final judgment in their Act 6. I prefer the way my Act 6 balances Act 2, and makes the gospel the central part of the whole drama.

1 CREATION

Parts of this chapter are adapted from my article "Theology and Ethics of the Land," *Transformation* 16, no. 3 (July 1, 1999): 81-86; and my book *The Mission of God: Unlocking the Bible's Grand Narrative* (Downers Grove, IL: InterVarsity Press, 2006).

[1]For a very readable, informative (and entertaining) introduction to the way the cultures of the ancient Near East thought about the cosmos and its origins, and how the biblical teaching both fits within that world and yet is radically distinct as well, see Robin A. Parry, *The Biblical Cosmos: A Pilgrim's Guide to the Weird and Wonderful World of the Bible* (Eugene, OR: Cascade, 2014).

[2]*Ontology* has to do with the nature of being or reality, the essence of things, what anything is in itself. Our statement means that the *being or essence* of God is utterly distinct from the *being or essence* of the universe. God is Creat*or*. All else is creat*ed*.

[3]See especially John Walton, *The Lost World of Genesis One: Ancient Cosmology and the Origins Debate* (Downers Grove, IL: InterVarsity Press, 2009); Greg Beale, *The Temple and the Church's Mission: A Biblical Theology of the Dwelling Place of God* (Downers Grove, IL: InterVarsity Press, 2004).

[4]Or, as I saw in the bathroom of a Marriott hotel room, "We are all guests on this planet." It did not specify, however, *whose* guests we are.

[5]When two "let us" clauses follow each other, the second can be seen as the purpose of the first. For example, "Let's take a break now and let's get

some coffee." You do the first in order to be able to do the second. In the same way, when God says, "Let us make mankind in our image . . . and let them rule over the other creatures," the first is what enables and equips us to do the second.

[6]It is important to note that the Hebrew word translated "helper" in Genesis 2:18 does not imply any inferiority (like some kind of mere personal assistant). The word is most often used in the Old Testament for God himself, whose help we certainly need but who is hardly our inferior. And the word translated by the NIV as "suitable" means "alongside" or "equivalent to." The text is stressing the matching equality of the man and the woman in the creational task assigned by God to humanity as the image of God.

[7]For a helpful explanation and discussion of these points, see Robert S. White, *Who Is to Blame? Disasters, Nature and Acts of God* (Grand Rapids: Monarch, 2014).

2 ABRAHAM

[1]The NIV says, "even though" instead of "for." But its footnote is probably right—the word should be translated "for." God *knows* that humans will continue to sin, and *therefore* he chooses to make this commitment. God's grace is there not so much in spite of human sin, but precisely because of it.

[2]I have surveyed the great sweep and universal implications of God's promise to Abraham and Sarah throughout the whole Bible in *The Mission of God: Unlocking the Bible's Grand Narrative* (Downers Grove, IL: Inter-Varsity Press, 2006), 191-264; and *The Mission of God's People* (Grand Rapids: Zondervan, 2010), 63-95.

[3]I survey the rich meanings of *blessing* in the Bible (to whet your appetite: it is creational, relational, missional, historical, covenantal, and ethical) in *Salvation Belongs to Our God: Celebrating the Bible's Central Story* (Downers Grove, IL: InterVarsity Press, 2008), 58-89.

[4]Here are a few more, when you have time to read them: Psalms 67; 72:17; 87; 96; 117.

[5]Richard Bauckham, *Bible and Mission: Christian Witness in a Postmodern World* (Grand Rapids: Baker Academic, 2003), 35-36.

3 EXODUS

[1]For a much fuller exploration of Old Testament law as a whole and its ethical relevance for Christians, see my *Old Testament Ethics for the People of God* (Downers Grove, IL: InterVarsity Press, 2004). In relation

to the points made in this section, see further *How to Preach and Teach the Old Testament for All It's Worth* (Grand Rapids: Zondervan, 2016); also published as *Sweeter than Honey: Preaching the Old Testament* (Carlisle, UK: Langham Preaching Resources, 2016) , chap. 9.

4 David

[1]For a much deeper wrestling with these issues, see my *The God I Don't Understand: Reflections on Tough Questions of Faith* (Grand Rapids: Zondervan, 2008), part 2, "What About the Canaanites?," 73-108. Two of the best full books on the subject are by Paul Copan, *Is God a Moral Monster: Making Sense of the Old Testament God* (Grand Rapids: Baker, 2011); and *Did God Really Command Genocide: Coming to Terms with the Justice of God* (Grand Rapids: Baker, 2014).

5 Prophets

[1]Some of the material in the sections below is condensed and adapted from my book *How to Preach and Teach the Old Testament for All It's Worth* (Grand Rapids: Zondervan, 2016), also published as *Sweeter than Honey: Preaching the Old Testament* (Carlisle, UK: Langham Preaching Resources, 2016), chaps. 11-12. Used with permission.

[2]In our Bibles, Daniel comes between Ezekiel and the Book of the Twelve. That makes sixteen. But in the Hebrew canon, Daniel is not listed among the Prophets but among the Writings. That's why I refer to fifteen books: three Major Prophets, plus twelve Minor Prophets.

6 Gospel

[1]I have discussed the topic of God, Israel, and the nations much more fully in Christopher J. H. Wright, *The Mission of God: Unlocking the Bible's Grand Narrative* (Downers Grove, IL: InterVarsity Press, 2006), chap. 14.

7 Psalms and Wisdom

[1]Some of the material in this chapter is condensed and adapted from *How To Preach and Teach the Old Testament For All It's Worth* (Grand Rapids: Zondervan, 2016), also published as *Sweeter than Honey: Preaching the Old Testament* (Carlisle, UK: Langham Preaching Resources, 2016), chaps. 13-15. Used with permission.

[2]Hymns of praise include Psalms 8; 33; 47; 65–66; 100; 103–4; 111; 113; 117; 145–50.

[3]Thanksgiving psalms include Psalms 18; 30; 32; 34; 40; 66; 92; 116; 118; 138.

[4]Individual laments include Psalms 3; 6; 13; 22; 31; 39; 42; 57; 71; 73; 88; 142. Community laments include Psalms 44; 74; 80; 91; 94; 137.

[5]Psalms of Zion include Psalms 46; 48; 76; 84; 87; 122; 125.

[6]In the book of Psalms they are called Songs of Ascents, because people literally had to go up to Jerusalem since it was set on a hill. They include Psalms 120–34.

[7]Royal psalms include Psalms 2; 18; 20–21; 45; 72; 89; 101; 110; 132. Psalms of Yahweh's kingship include Psalms 96–99.

[8]The word *meditates* here does not just mean silent, inner thinking (as it does in English). In Hebrew it usually means reading aloud (alone or in company), or reciting the words of Scripture, again and again. It is an active engagement with the text, chewing it over, as we might say.

[9]Examples of these wisdom psalms, or teaching psalms, include Psalms 36–37; 49; 73; 112; 127–28; 133.

[10]If this book had been called *The Old Testament in Eight Sentences*, I would have made this one my final chapter.

SCRIPTURE INDEX

ALSO BY CHRISTOPHER J. H. WRIGHT

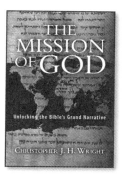

The Mission of God
978-0-8308-5213-0

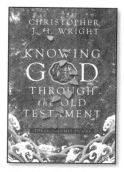

**Knowing God Through
the Old Testament**
978-0-8308-5243-7

The Message of Jeremiah
978-0-8308-2439-7

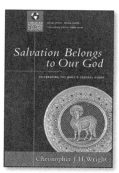

**Salvation Belongs
to Our God**
978-0-8308-3306-1

**Cultivating the Fruit
of the Spirit**
978-0-8308-4498-2

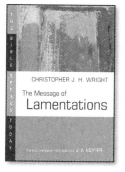

**The Message of
Lamentations**
978-0-8308-2441-0

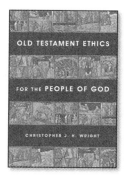

**Old Testament Ethics for
the People of God**
978-0-8308-2778-7

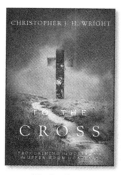

To the Cross
978-0-8308-4499-9

The Message of Ezekiel
978-0-8308-2425-0

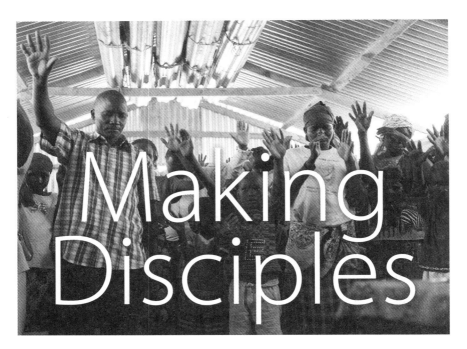

Making Disciples

Around the World — Christianity is exploding with growth in numbers

Yet — Believers are struggling to grow in Christ

That's Why Langham Exists

Our Vision

To see churches in the Majority World equipped for mission and growing to maturity in Christ through the ministry of pastors and leaders who believe, teach and live by the Word of God.

www.langham.org

FOUNDED BY JOHN STOTT